I0210808

Incarnational Life

Incarnational Life

Being Light to All Creation

Otis E. Hamm Jr.

WIPF & STOCK · Eugene, Oregon

INCARNATIONAL LIFE
Being Light to All Creation

Copyright © 2017 Otis E. Hamm Jr. All rights reserved. Except for brief quotations in critical publications or reviews, no part of this book may be reproduced in any manner without prior written permission from the publisher. Write: Permissions, Wipf and Stock Publishers, 199 W. 8th Ave., Suite 3, Eugene, OR 97401.

Wipf & Stock
An Imprint of Wipf and Stock Publishers
199 W. 8th Ave., Suite 3
Eugene, OR 97401

www.wipfandstock.com

PAPERBACK ISBN: 978-1-5326-0901-5
HARDCOVER ISBN: 978-1-5326-0903-9
EBOOK ISBN: 978-1-5326-0902-2

Manufactured in the U.S.A.   JUNE 9, 2017

This work is dedicated to the love of my life, the one given to me by God to share in each other's journey. My ever-encouraging wife, Veta, has always been my spark. I am truly blessed to be loved by and in love with such a magnificent lady. I love you, Poopsie.

Contents

Preface

WHAT EXACTLY DID ST. Bonaventure mean when he said:

> Let your love lead your steps to Jesus wounded, to Jesus crowned with thorns, to Jesus fastened upon the gibbet of the cross. Not only see in His hands the print of the nails, not only put finger into the place of the nails, not only put your hand into His side, but enter with your whole being through the door of His side into Jesus' heart itself. There transformed into Christ by your burning love for the Crucified, pierced by the nails of the fear of God, wounded by the spear of superabounding love, transfixed by the sword of intimate compassion, seek nothing, desire nothing, wish for no consolation, other than to be able to die with Christ on the cross. Then you may cry out, "With Christ, I am nailed to the cross. It is now no longer I that lives, but Christ lives in me."[1]

This extremely personal and yet, nonetheless, profoundly corporate expression of Christian life is completely relational in essence. The premise of this book is to explore the essence of humanity's relational existence with the Creator, and in particular, the life that emerges from a nurtured relationship such as St. Bonaventure describes. What does it mean to die to one's self and take up the

1. Delio, *Franciscan Prayer*, 115–16.

cross of Christ? What does it mean when he says that "it is now no longer I that lives, but Christ lives in me"?

For so many Christians spiritual life begins and ultimately ends with the initial conversion experience. However, there is much more to the journey than the emotional moments shared during a relevant worship service or other form of meaningful event that captures one's attention for a few brief seconds. Our Creator desires so much more from us in a relationship than a fleeting moment of ecstasy, which is what St. Teresa of Avila warned her sisters about as they too wished for more moments of just such an experience. The spiritual life is more than ecstasy and rapturous moments that pass nearly as quickly as they emerge. The spiritual life is one in which the true essence, the image of Christ, delivers itself from the vessel—us—into the world and becomes light. Humanity, in every sense, is here to be the embodiment of Christ. This brief work will help the reader discover the practicality of such a statement and engage in practices that will enhance the relationship one has with Christ.

St. Bonaventure portrays an image of the journey one might traverse as a Christian; one that has many twists and turns. A journey that often has as many questions as it does answers, and at times even produces periods of doubt. In the end, the hope is that the journey leads one to the identity of the true self, one that is self-emptied, one that truly is the best image of Christ that she or he can manifest. One that sees the world as sister and brother with nothing but love for all and a willingness to give the shirt, feed the hungry, and take care of the sick. This is what incarnational life is and what this writer wishes to help convey.

Otis E. Hamm
2016

Chapter 1

Discovery

The lover was asked to whom he belonged?
He answered, "To love."
"What are you made of?" "Of love."
"Who gave birth to you?" "Love."
"Where were you born?" "In love."
"Who brought you up?" "Love."
"How do you live?" "By love."
"What is your name?" "Love."
"Where do you come from?" "From love."
"Where are you going?" "To love."
"Where are you now?" "In love."
"Have you anything other than love?"
"Yes, I have faults and wrongs against my beloved."
"Is there pardon in your beloved?"
The lover said that in his beloved were mercy and justice,
and that he therefore lived between fear and hope.

—RAMÓN LULL[1]

---

1. Lull, *The Book of the Lover*, as quoted by Delio, *Franciscan Prayer*, 17.

RAMÓN LULL'S BEAUTIFUL POEM delivers a thirteenth-century image of the relationship one encounters with the Creator. This image speaks of great love and wondrous life. A sense of a marvelous journey comes into play as the philosopher's question is pondered: "Where are you going?" The image continues with the ideal of forgiveness that accompanies this profound love combined with a hope for life everlasting. Is that not the essence of Christianity? Exploration is the key to excitement as well as awareness, so let's explore.

In the first few lines of the poem Lull explores creation, implicitly human creation, at least so it would seem. However, one must remember that Lull was a Franciscan and therefore creation is all of creation. For now let's consider the concept of humanity and her relationship as created beings with her Creator. In order to do so, one must review the sources. Our first source comes from the Scriptures, Genesis 1–3. Within the walls of these three chapters we find two narratives of creation, each of differing time periods and authorship. The first often used as liturgy in the early Jewish tradition speaking to the majesty of the Creator, while the second narrative speaks more profoundly to the relationship between Creator and creation. Much more could be stated regarding the exegetical positions regarding these two narratives, but the effort here is to delve into the spiritual rather than the solely academic.

That stated, concerning the first narrative one can conclude the sovereignty of God is clearly at play. God spoke and it was so, and it was good. This is important on many levels:

1. It speaks to the character of God.
2. It speaks to the power of God.
3. It alludes to the relationship between creation and Creator—dependent.
4. It speaks to the relationships of creation—male and female—and gives them dominion.

Concerning the character or nature of God one can certainly gather that God is all-powerful. When God spoke it, it happened.

Not only did it happen, it was good. I'm reminded of the movie *Bruce Almighty* and the funny line that Jim Carrey often spoke, "It's gooood." In some abstract fashion the movie got it right—God is good and all God created, *all*, is good. Sometimes it's difficult to grasp that concept. Our tendencies are to pay attention to the news, which feeds us with the sensational most negative and depressing images of the day to cloud our minds and disrupt our hearts. This disruption leads to a confused spirit that sometimes fails to see the good or stops searching for it altogether. The nature of God is more than just a sound bite. Discovering the nature/character of God is the ability to see and hear the awful things that take place in the world and rather than run and hide in one form or another (for some this is turning the channel, for others this is blaming a political party, for others this is blaming a religious tradition, and still others, blaming God), have the ability to see Christ in the event and/or be able to take a position of helper. Knowing that the very Creator of all is within and always with, expecting creation to act rather than to simply stand by with disdain and watch.

The relationship between Creator and creation within the first narrative is one of dependency. The sovereignty of God is clearly portrayed as the focal point. For humanity this means that we must realize that our lives are not our own, they are that of the One who created all. An often-quoted passage (albeit not fully quoted) from *The Confessions of St. Augustine of Hippo* reads: "Nevertheless, to praise you is the desire of man, a little piece of your creation. You stir man to take pleasure in praising you, because you have made us for yourself, and our heart is restless until it rests in you."[2] Here, Augustine carries forth a notion from the philosopher Plotinus whose work regarding the One was an early approach to the nature of spirituality. Augustine is expanding the idea by describing the dynamics of desire, praise, and restlessness. Desire is a topic that will be expanded upon in chapter 4, but suffice it to say that desire implies the need for humanity to be in relationship with the Creator. It is within the essence of that need that dependency emerges. As the need becomes fulfilled through

2. Augustine, *Confessions*, I, i, 4.

such things as praise, a soothing of the desire moves into place for the moment; however, the moment is fleeting, which creates a restlessness spurred by the desire to engage the Creator in a more life-sustaining manner. We become hungry for more. Our relationship with the Creator is one of true dependency, but not in some negative fashion, but rather one that transforms us into the image and likeness of God—something by ourselves we are simply not capable of achieving.

The ideal of human dominion is often one that is misunderstood. Humanity, in her dependent state, is not lord and master over creation, but rather caretaker. Creation, meaning all that exists other than humanity, is the responsibility of humanity. It is our task to care for this universe as our Creator cares for us. Both creation narratives imply this basic concept of dominion *with* rather than *over*. The more humanity relinquishes herself to God the better we understand that creation, all of creation, is good.

As we ponder the second narrative, these concepts emerge:

1. The humanity dynamic.

2. The essence and nature of relational being.

3. A much closer Creator.

The second narrative of creation delivers a different depiction of the nature of God within creation. God is seemingly more attuned with creation, seeking to satisfy the needs of creation in a relational fashion. God is portraying what some would refer to as a human nature. Consider a few thousand years in the future and the man that is Jesus, he is God incarnate walking the areas of Palestine the same as any other man or women fully human. Jesus ate, drank, put on his clothes and did everything else related to being human. Jesus also healed the blind, the deaf, and raised the dead, displaying his divine nature. Therefore, Jesus was both fully human and fully divine. Why then, would it be so difficult to grasp that within the two creation narratives we find a Creator displaying the same two natures? The second narrative is profoundly relational. In this narrative one can certainly gather that the nature of God is that of a caring, loving

Creator seeking relationship with creation. What's more, the two are inseparable. According to Walter Brueggemann, the phrase "Creator creates creation" is a grammatically significant affirmation that "Creator is not disinterested and the creation is not autonomous."[3] Building on the tone of Brueggemann, the realization that God is interested in us in the capacity of being in a relationship, can be quite fascinating and at times even a bit nerve-racking.

Discovering there is more to the Christian life than one emotional experience is quite earth-shattering. The idea that there are multiple conversion experiences within the Christian journey is often a bit of new news to many longtime Christians, but allow me to share a piece from a wonderful Trappist monk—Thomas Merton:

> How the valley awakes. At two-fifteen in the morning there are no sounds except in the monastery: the bells ring, the office begins. Outside, nothing, except perhaps a bullfrog saying "Om" in the creek or in the guesthouse pond. Some nights he is in Samadhi; there is not even an "Om." The mysterious and uninterrupted whooping of the whippoorwill begins about three, these mornings. He is not always near. Sometimes there are two whooping together, perhaps a mile away in the woods in the east.
>
> The first chirps of the waking day birds mark the point *vierge* of the dawn under a sky as yet without real light, a moment of awe and inexpressible innocence, when the Father in perfect silence opens their eyes. They begin to speak to him, not with fluent song, but with an awakening question that is their dawn state, their state at the point *vierge*. Their condition asks if it is time for them to "be." He answers "yes." Then they one by one wake up, and become birds. They manifest themselves as birds, beginning to sing. Presently they will be fully themselves and even fly.
>
> Meanwhile, the most wonderful moment of the day is that when creation in its innocence asks permission to "be" once again, as it did on the first morning that ever was.[4]

---

3. Brueggemann, *Genesis*, 17.
4. Merton, *Conjectures*, 127–28.

As one traverses the many dynamics of this beautiful bit of prose one can gather that Merton is infatuated with the early morning processes of nature and how creation comes alive. From the Om of the frog to the gentle whooping of the whippoorwill, creation is coming to life as if for the very first time. The birds are chirping and asking permission to simply "be." Merton is not only describing what he is seeing and hearing within the created nature of the woods of the Kentucky hills, he is also contemplating the essence of humanity. The virgin day for humanity is every day. Every day we can expect God to wake us anew and to be present within our lives. When we arise with God recalling that unlike us God never sleeps, we can begin the day with a sense of purpose knowing that our Creator has made us with intent. What has passed, has passed today, is a virgin day with new opportunities to be light, to live out the incarnate.

Take note of the manner in which Merton carefully listens to creation speak and how Merton finds God in all he hears. This is one of the challenges we face. How do we see Christ in creation? How in fact, do we see Christ in others? Perhaps the answer lies within this profound question: How do we see Christ within ourselves? The ideal of discovery is one that looks deeply into the self to find the measure of the heart. I recall an extremely meaningful statement made by one of my graduate school professors: "We must learn to think with our hearts and to feel with our brains."[5] A very Franciscan comment from a Franciscan teaching a course concerning the cosmic Christ. Nonetheless, the statement is relevant for our purposes. As one discovers the depths of her or his relationship with God one begins to encounter a paradigm shift in thinking. This is consistent with the concept of loosing one's false self and finding one's true self. The supposition of this concept is that we begin to realize that there is so much more to our relationship with God, but in order to reveal the image of God in more depth, we must begin to peel away the layers of our old natures. We must truly grasp the understanding of dying to self, which creates a different mind-set. We move from the "I" to "thou" mentality; "It is no longer I but Christ who dwells in me."

5. Ilia Delio, graduate school lecture (2009).

At no point is the relationship meant to be forced; God is not interested in a thug approach to salvation. When teaching New and Old Testament survey courses, students would often ask about how the Bible defines salvation. My response was usually something like: well it's not something created out of fear. God's not the thug on the corner waiting to jack your car and jump into the backseat. Point a gun at your head and tell you where to go and how fast to go to get there. No, God desires a loving relationship, one that you choose to be involved with as a member of God's family. Of course there would always be a couple of students that would disagree, stating that their pastor always taught that they should fear God. I suppose that fearing a loving God is something one might consider to a degree, but I think revering a loving God is much better. The bottom line is that God has provided humanity with a choice, free will, to choose whether or not to be in relationship. The cross of Christ was the most vulnerable act of Jesus' life. At the cross Jesus freely gave his life with no strings or expectations beyond offering the sacrifice for humanity in order that humanity might have an opportunity to choose. The beauty of the cross is just that, Jesus never commanded that all will follow, or that all will become, he only provided a way—the choice belongs to humanity. That's the vulnerability of the cross.

As we continue to consider the dynamics of discovery and focus on the aspects of conversion as they relate to not only seeking a more intimate relationship with God, but also beginning to understand that that relationship is meant to be shared with the community, ponder this quote from Ronald Rolheiser: "How do we as Christians, walk this earth as gods? As co-creators? As persons, in God's image and likeness, who are trying to help God save the planet and everything on it? How do we fulfill our God-given vocations? By being part of God's ongoing incarnation."[6] Rolheiser describes what a Christian journey is: *imitatio Christi* (imitation of Christ). The vocation of the Christian community is exactly what Rolheiser declares—to live an incarnate life. Easier said than done in most cases. We need a little help. Discovering the essence of

6. Rolheiser, *Holy Longing*, 70.

our own existence can be an eye-opening experience. Discovering the essence of God's existence can be a life-changing experience. Nonetheless, the path has been laid before us and with the help of our Lord the journey will be exciting. Realizing that the words of Augustine cited earlier, "our hearts will not rest oh Lord until they rest in you," can actually apply to the nature of God—God's heart may not rest until it rests in us! Now that's something to consider. Imagine what the love of God truly means. Not only did God create us, God also gave the life of the incarnate Christ for us and now awaits reciprocation. Not a physical death on our parts, but an inner death to ourselves so that we can live out the image that we have been created in—God's. In the next chapter we will explore the meaning of the phrase "created in the image and likeness of God." From this point, move to the reflection questions.

Reflection Questions

1. Reread Ramón Lull's poem and discuss your take on its meaning.

2. How do the two creation narratives relate to your own image of God and your own relationship with God?

3. Discuss what discovery means and how it relates to your journey.

4. How did you read Merton's ideal of the virgin day?

Chapter 2

The Interior Challenge

You called, you cried out loud and shattered my deafness. You were radiant and resplendent, you put to flight my blindness. You were fragrant, and I drew in my breath, and I pant for you. I tasted and now I hunger and thirst for you. You touched me, and I am set on fire to attain the peace which is yours.[1]

St. Augustine's words can present quite a quandary for us as we encounter the early church father's piety. His journey leads him toward a richer relationship with Christ built upon desire. St. Augustine is alluding to the interior life as engaged by the individual seeking more from God than the emotional reactions of the temporal. The interior life is a constant building and refreshing of relationship between the individual and Christ. At best, this relationship seeks to provide a death of sorts to the selfish existence of the human nature and life to the selfless existence of the incarnate Christ. The ultimate outcome is found within the exterior manifestation of the incarnate Christ as the bright light of Christ alive, well, and serving humanity through the ongoing work and life of

---

1. Augustine, *Confessions*, X, xxvii, 201.

the individual. Thinking of life in this manner and beginning to embrace one's relationship with Christ in such a passionate fashion can be quite the challenge. This chapter attempts to provide the reader with examples of the interior life made manifest by exterior examples of Christ living and being within community.

In the early formative years and for the more seasoned Christian, as well, the term "incarnate Christ" usually connotes the well-known birth narratives of the gospels and the prophecies of the Christ child from the Old Testament. To consider something more intimate than that, something more personal, an individual concept in fact can present challenges. Many are taught that once one becomes a "believer," the Holy Spirit dwells within and guides one through life. Others come to a similar understanding in a more formal catechetical process involving the sacrament of confirmation that continues throughout life in the sacrament of the Eucharist (which will be explored at another point in this text). Still others arrive at this understanding by an emotional experience after a profession of faith. While these are not an exhaustive grouping of examples, they do serve to provide the majority of Christian experiences within today's setting, each expressing discernible validity. Exploring the essence of the incarnate Christ as part and parcel to an individual's spirituality is taking the relationship a bit further. Recognizing that God desires more from us than a simple "yes" when asked if we would like to have him living in our heart; or moving beyond the borders of Sunday school and discovering the giftedness that one has been blessed with and then, discerning the field or even fields to work moves us beyond the comfortable and into the arena of selflessness.

Regardless of one's faith tradition within Christendom the term "incarnation" applies. So let's provide a bit of clarity by way of definition to this classical term. Rolheiser quotes John Shea regarding incarnation: "Jesus is not a law to be obeyed or a model to be imitated, but a presence to be seized and acted upon."[2] Shea touches on the essence of incarnation—presence. In the most basic of terms incarnation is the true presence of Christ within one's be-

2. Rolheiser, *Holy Longing*, 74, quoting from Shea, *Stories of Faith*.

ing. Notice the term "being" is used in place of the term "life." In one sense life is fleeting, being is infinite. The presence of Christ is determinable by a myriad of events in one's journey with Jesus:

- Worship
- Music
- Prayer
- Giving
- Word
- Sacraments
- Response
- Being sent forth
- Spiritual disciplines
- Prayer—various forms: breath, office, *lectio divina*, centering
- Journaling
- Labyrinth
- Rosary
- Examen

Certainly not an exhaustive list, but nonetheless a list that can begin a formative dialogue regarding the presence of Jesus within one's being.

Biblical Dynamics of Incarnation

Prior to exploring the aforementioned list perhaps a venture into the biblical dynamics of incarnation would prove to be beneficial. Arguably the most prudent text to consider is John 1:1–14:

> In the beginning was the Word, and the Word was with God, and the Word was God. He was in the beginning with God. All things came into being through him, and without him not one thing came into being. What has come into being in him was life, and the life was the light

of all people. The light shines in the darkness, and the darkness did not overcome it.

There was a man sent from God, whose name was John. He came as a witness to testify to the light, so that all might believe through him. He himself was not the light, but he came to testify to the light. The true light, which enlightens everyone, was coming into the world.

He was in the world, and the world came into being through him; yet the world did not know him. He came to what was his own, and his own people did not accept him. But to all who received him, who believed in his name, he gave power to become children of God, who were born, not of blood or of the will of the flesh or of the will of man, but of God.

And the Word became flesh and lived among us, and we have seen his glory, the glory as of a father's only son, full of grace and truth. (NRSV)

In this gospel text, the only one that proclaims the birth narrative in such cosmic terms, Jesus is defined as being with God from the beginning—creation itself. The text is one of the more challenging found within the four gospels. It forgoes a classical birth narrative as well as any discernible John the Baptist narrative, but rather informs the listener and reader of regional events and eternal possibilities. The Word refers not only to the Greek term *logos*—the literal "word"—but in this instance is meant as a christological term providing in one sense salvific connotations, but also earthbound eschatological means to a way of life. God, in all sovereignty and glory has chosen to dwell among creation and provide the word in the flesh—incarnation. The word is not simply spoken, but lived out in the being of Jesus who walked, talked, and was among the peoples of the day. Jesus did not simply lead by example; he also expressed a desire to be in relationship with all of creation.

To further explore the previous quote from Rolheiser, "What Jesus wants of us is that we undergo his presence so as to enter into a community of life and celebration with him. Jesus, as John Shea says, is not a law to be obeyed or a model to be imitated, but a presence to be seized and acted upon,"[3] one can gather a few concepts. First, a community of life represents the entirety of humanity and the solemnity of the individual all at the same time. Within the confines of the individual is a vast array of thoughts and desires, wants and wishes, false and true selves, in this respect a community. However, in a more literal than metaphysical sense, community relates to those whom we encounter—humanity. So how do we perceive the presence of Jesus in these two dynamics, and within celebration of him as well? Presence is the key. Certainly celebration seems the most fantastic element with an absolute measure of ease and accomplishment.

Celebration is not always what one thinks it is—formal worship. Celebration can be a myriad of things:

- Praising God in a car.
- Praying any place and in any form.
- A simple smile.
- An extended hand.
- A bow.
- A wave.
- Any warm gesture.
- A random act of kindness.
- An article of clothing.
- Jewelry.
- A tattoo.

Informal celebration takes on many forms and relates to many lifestyles and many people. The wonderful thing about creation is that we have not all been created with a cookie cutter, meaning that we are all not the same and our images of God are all not the same and therefore, our mannerisms related to celebrating God are different. That does not mean any one form is greater or lesser than another.

3. Ibid.

Celebration is celebration. Loving God and acknowledging God's presence in one's life is a beautiful thing period.

Regarding formal worship, those who lead worship as well as those who participate/attend must be prepared—arrived prepared—to experience the presence of God. Thus, all must have the presence of God within them. Seems simple enough, but can be rather complicated. Some might suggest that it is not necessary to have the presence of God within in order to worship God. The argument is somewhat valid, but can be challenged with Genesis 1:26:

> Then God said, "Let us make humankind in our image, according to our likeness; and let them have dominion over the fish of the sea, and over the birds of the air, and over the cattle, and over all the wild animals of the earth, and over every creeping thing that creeps upon the earth." (NRSV)

The writer clearly exclaims that all of humanity is created in the image and likeness of God. Therefore, all have the ability to arrive at worship prepared for the presence of God. Although, if the statement is too difficult to embrace it could be revised to read all who know God should arrive prepared to experience the presence of God. The hope and intent is not to get tangled in theology, but rather to move toward awareness of the presence of God in our lives.

Formally, the Eucharist provides another point of reception of the presence of Christ. For those who consider the Eucharist in a sacramental sense, the body and blood of Christ are very real and present during the sacrament. Each element, once consecrated, becomes the body of Christ, the bread of life and the blood of Christ, the cup of salvation. Those affirming this theology find the presence of the incarnate Christ at each service and leave the service with a feeling of fresh love and sense of reflecting the light of Christ to the world. Others, who consider the Lord's Supper in a more symbolic manner, also find the presence of Christ within the service, but not in as much of a literal sense. They too leave the service—which for most happens more infrequently—with a renewed sense of belonging and hope. One commonality in both of these examples is the *koinonia* that forms during the time that the Eucharist is enjoyed. A true sense of fellowship, even community, emerges as persons take part together in joy and humility.

Through awareness/discovery God's presence in our lives becomes more real than ever. It is exactly that presence that allows us to present the incarnate Christ to the community we engage daily. Learning to cope with the internal community and discover the true self is somewhat of a lifelong experience. Thomas Merton wrote rather extensively of the journey from false self to true self and the struggle to become the purpose in which we have been created to become. This excerpt from *Conjectures of a Guilty Bystander* provides an interesting and yet profound interpretation of incarnation:

> How the valley awakes. At two-fifteen in the morning there are no sounds except in the monastery: the bells ring, the office begins. Outside, nothing, except perhaps a bullfrog saying "Om" in the creek or in the guesthouse pond. Some nights he is in Samadhi; there is not even an "Om." The mysterious and uninterrupted whooping of the whippoorwill begins about three, these mornings. He is not always near. Sometimes there are two whooping together, perhaps a mile away in the woods in the east.
>
> The first chirps of the waking day birds mark the point *vierge* of the dawn under a sky as yet without real light, a moment of awe and inexpressible innocence, when the Father in perfect silence opens their eyes. They begin to speak to him, not with fluent song, but with an awakening question that is their dawn state, their state at the point *vierge*. Their condition asks if it is time for them to "be." He answers "yes." Then they one by one wake up, and become birds. They manifest themselves as birds, beginning to sing. Presently they will be fully themselves and even fly.
>
> Meanwhile, the most wonderful moment of the day is that when creation in its innocence asks permission to "be" once again, as it did on the first morning that ever was.[4]

Merton speaks to the dawn of a new day and the life of all creation as being that of something new. It is a virgin day, one that has not occurred before and should be considered as one that belongs to

4. Merton, *Conjectures*, 127–28.

both creation and Creator working together. Drawing upon an awakening within, which on the surface is an individual matter. A matter, that simultaneously exemplifies the merger of heart, soul, and mind with Creator-God in a beautiful symphony balanced and ever evolving. Permitting oneself to engage God in an intimate fashion rather than an imperialistic one permits the Spirit to manifest itself internally, creating room every day for expansion. Our natural self, that is selfish by nature, dissipates and our true self emerges. The danger is that our very human nature attempts to reinforce the false self, driving out the true self through a myriad of temptations. Realizing the nature of God is the greatest key to understanding the battle being waged within. Merton would have us arise to greet the day as a new creation, not only metaphysically but in the flesh as well. Each day is a gift to all creation to be enjoyed and experienced in unison with the purpose of the Creator living out the incarnate Christ that dwells within.

Another biblical text that points toward incarnation is Colossians 1:15–20:

> He is the image of the invisible God, the firstborn of all creation; for in him all things in heaven and on earth were created, things visible and invisible, whether thrones or dominions or rulers or powers—all things have been created through him and for him. He himself is before all things, and in him all things hold together. He is the head of the body, the church; he is the beginning, the firstborn from the dead, so that he might come to have first place in everything. For in him all the fullness of God was pleased to dwell, and through him God was pleased to reconcile to himself all things, whether on earth or in heaven, by making peace through the blood of his cross. (NRSV)

Perhaps one of the more debatable christological hymns of the New Testament, this Pauline text presents the image of Christ as firstborn of all creation. For centuries scholars have attempted to exegete this text describing it in various manners: Gnostic revision, Hebraic revision from Genesis 1, to Wisdom with redemptive dynamics. With these three presuppositions in mind, the second and third receiving the most attention, incarnation from another worldly (God thing) viewpoint seems viable. Certainly one can discern the similarities between the hymn and Genesis 1. The phraseology—*before all things* and *in the beginning*; *is the beginning* and *in the beginning*—supports some reference, if not parallel, to the Genesis text. The question is, to what end? Wisdom and *logos*, which are the redemptive dynamic of the text, are supported through other biblical texts, such as:

> Proverbs 8:27–31: When he established the heavens, I was there, when he drew a circle on the face of the deep, when he made firm the skies above, when he established the fountains of the deep, when he assigned to the sea its limit, so that the waters might not transgress his command, when he marked out the foundations of the earth, then I was beside him, like a master worker; and I was daily his delight, rejoicing before him always, rejoicing in his inhabited world and delighting in the human race. (NRSV)

and,

> Sirach 24:5–6: Alone I compassed the vault of heaven and traversed the depths of the abyss. Over waves of the sea, over all the earth and over every people and nation I have held sway. (NRSV)

Christ is the firstborn and recognized as Wisdom, one of the Greek renderings for God (*Sophia*). The *logos* (word) announces peace through redemption—Christ, who is God incarnate. The *logos* also reveals the regenerated life of the redeemed—the incarnate Christ living within humanity being the light to the world.[5]

The nature of Jesus in this hymn is that of the incarnate God, who has always been—the first of all creation. The One who has come into creation with purpose through love to provide a means of redemption and a path forward by regeneration in a continued relationship. This relationship never ceases to grow but often finds itself in need of repair. As one considers these biblical texts and the ideal of incarnation I'd like to present a voice that left this world in 1955.

5. Lincoln, *New Interpreter's*, 597–605.

Another Voice

French-born Jesuit Pierre Teilhard de Chardin has a very intriguing viewpoint regarding incarnation. Teilhard's work was well ahead of its time and met with great resistance from the church. Today, efforts are being made to revitalize his work and bring it forward in attempts to further understand as well as relate to his spirituality. One of the foremost scholars broaching an effort with this project is Ilia Delio, OSF, a Franciscan sister who last served as senior fellow in science and theology at Woodstock Theological Center, Georgetown University, where she remains on staff and also lectures around the country. In her book *The Emergent Christ*, Delio refers to Teilhard often, noting his distinctive spirituality as well as his scientific ideology, carefully exploring the symmetry of the two. Regarding Teilhard's viewpoints of evolution and creative union she writes:

> Teilhard described the incarnation as "creative union," a process of immanent unification in which Christ is in the process of being created by the gradual unification of multiplicity. Thus "creation" is to be not at the "beginning" of the world but at its "end." Creation emerges with evolution as lower level entities become higher level entities with a persistent emergence of novelty whereby each unification results in new being.[6]

To gain a better understanding of this quote perhaps a brief excurses into the ideology of creation from Teilhard's vantage point would be prudent. Classically, creation has been considered to be an act of free will on God's part either by way of desire or by way of intellect; however, Teilhard contended that creation was integral to God; something not to complete God's being, but rather to fulfill God's act of union.[7] God works through humanity as the incarnate person of Christ (Teilhard often referred to Jesus as the Omega Christ; present in all things). The "union" is the relationship between humanity and Christ, which is being created and

6. Delio, *Emergent Christ*, 47.
7. Ibid., 46.

fulfilled throughout time moving toward a new creation described as the "end" or as some would call it the return of Christ or end of this world. For Teilhard the end is the beginning brought about through relationship with Christ. Delio explains it this way:

> Rather than following the classic physical construct of the many flowing from the One [God] (a devolution or thinning out of being), Teilhard posited that the One flows from the many (a building up toward the fullness of being). The involvement of God in evolution through creative union means that everything happens as though the One were formed by successive unifications of the multiple, and as though the One were more perfect the more perfectly it centralized under itself a larger multiple. God revealed everywhere as a universal milieu (surroundings, environment), only because God is the ultimate point upon which all realities converge.[8]

The ideal is less complicated than it seems; humanity, in Teilhard's view, is created to journey with God toward unity and finality. The journey involves Teilhard's concepts of evolution as it pertains to humanity and Christ (in a cosmic sense). Humanity's evolution is that of expressing the Christ within (incarnate) to the world. Being Christ to others and exposing the Christ in others. The journey is a means, relationally, to a beginning. That beginning is eternity. In no way does Teilhard deviate from Christian thought, quite the contrary, he moves far and away toward the ideal of Christian livelihood in concert with expressed relationship with Christ and engaged relationship with humanity. There is much more to Teilhard than these brief reflections—a book or two in the future perhaps—let it be said that he truly understood how to feel with his mind and think with his heart.

8. Ibid., 48.

To Wrap It Up

A bit oxymoronic to think that introducing an ideal like "incarnation" could be summed up in the confines of one chapter. A paradigm shift in thought and relationship is difficult to embrace no matter what evidence is presented. Incarnational living—allowing the Christ inside to become the Christ manifest—is no easy task. Perception is one of the most difficult boundaries to overcome when one is attempting to allow transformation in one's life. There is a simplicity to understanding incarnational living. An example provided by Rolheiser concerning a mother and her daughter comes to mind. The daughter was four years old and awoke one night extremely frightened, convinced that there were monsters in the darkness. All alone in her room, she quickly decided to run to her parents' room. Her mother did as any mother would do; she calmed her down and walked her back to her room. She turned on the light and assured the child that there were no monsters in her room and that she did not need to be afraid, because God was in the room with her. The child replied, "I know that God is here, but I need someone in this room who has some skin!"[9] Living out an incarnate life is as simple as putting some skin in the game. This young child only needed a live person in the room. For her that person represented God, meaning she saw Christ in her mother and that made her feel safe. There is rarely a day when at some point one does not have the opportunity become Christ to someone else. The difficulty is being aware of who we are, who dwells within, the opportunities of the day, and the actions of the heart that are done and left undone. Episcopal scholar Alan Jones wrote:

> In the waters of baptism we are reminded that we are not born in a vacuum, nor do we journey entirely alone (although loneliness is often part of the burden). Being reborn, being made alive, involves being born into a community. So there are strings attached to this adventure. Far from being the spiritual journey of the solitary

9. Rolheiser, *Holy Longing*, 76–77.

individual in search of God, it drags a people, a church, a nation, and the human race, along with it.[10]

Jones speaks of our connectedness to one another through baptism as our journeys are most certainly manifest representations of the incarnate Christ working within the community not only in an ecclesial setting, but also in an ecumenical one. By carefully reflecting upon and being mindful of the markers that derail us from the journey where we are created in God's image rather than "God created in ours," our journeys take on new life. As Merton resounds with his lovely prose it is not of our own, but that of our Creator where life happens, that we emanate the light of the incarnate within the world around us as each day begins anew and the Creator of all gives us breath, it is our path and God's dawn.

The following chapter will focus on the heart, and describe a heart that is emptied and ready to serve God.

Reflection Questions

1. Reflect upon the opening quote from Augustine.

2. What does Holy Communion mean to you? Where or how does Jesus' presence fit in?

3. Describe your understanding of the presence of God.

4. Respond to Teilhard.

10. Ibid., 111.

Chapter 3

Developing a Self-Emptying Heart

Do nothing from selfish ambition or conceit, but in humility regard others as better than yourselves. Let each of you look not to your own interests, but to the interests of others. Let the same mind be in you that was in Christ Jesus, who, though he was in the form of God, did not regard equality with God as something to be exploited, but emptied himself, taking the form of a slave, being born in human likeness. And being found in human form, he humbled himself and became obedient to the point of death—even death on a cross. Therefore God also highly exalted him and gave him the name that is above every name, so that at the name of Jesus every knee should bend, in heaven and on earth and under the earth, and every tongue should confess that Jesus Christ is Lord, to the glory of God the Father.

PHILIPPIANS 2:3-11

DIVING A BIT MORE deeply into the waters of christological hymnology in particularly, the hymn found in Philippians chapter 2 posits a sense of the cosmic nature of Scripture. Ronald Rolheiser states, "We are part of a universe, that part that has become conscious of itself, wherein everything yearns for something beyond just itself. We have in us spirit, soul, and what we do with that soul is our spirituality."[1] Rolheiser speaks of the energy, the desire, the *eros* within created humanity realizing, becoming aware of itself within the cosmos, knowing that being is relational, relational to the Creator. He continues by stating that "spirituality is about how we channel our *eros*."[2] Indeed, the process of channeling our fire, the fire that ignites the energy of our lifeblood, is vital to our spirituality. Writing about Franciscan prayer, and quoting St. Bonaventure, Ilia Delio presents:

> Whoever loves this death can see God because it is true beyond doubt that man [woman] will not see me and live. Let us, then, die and enter into the darkness; let us impose silence upon our cares, our desires and our imaginings. With Christ crucified let us pass out of this world to the Father so that when the Father is shown to us, we may say with Philip: It is enough for us. Let us hear with Paul: My grace is sufficient for you. Let us rejoice with David saying: My flesh and my heart have grown faint, You are the God of my heart, and the God that is my portion forever.[3]

This is the kenotic Christ, and the kenotic heart of Bonaventure exemplifies the essence of the fire declared by Rolheiser, a transformed, self-emptied life both of the cosmic Christ and the cosmic creation that leaves a humbled Bonaventure dependent and impoverished.

The Greek term *kenosis* must be clarified; C. Stephen Evans posits:

> Kenotic Christology is inspired by Philippians 2:6–11, which speaks of Christ as one who "being in very nature God" still "emptied himself" or "made himself nothing" (NIV). The Greek verb for "empty" (*kenoo*) is of course the source of the English noun "*kenosis*" and its adjective form "kenotic." This self-emptying does not stop with Christ's becoming human but goes to the extreme

1. Rolheiser, *Holy Longing*, 18.

2. Ibid., 11.

3. Delio, *Franciscan Prayer*, 177–78.

of "taking the very nature of a servant" and becoming
"obedient to death, even on a cross."[4]

From this position *kenosis* is understood as more than the incarnation of Christ, it encompasses the life work and death-work of
the Creator. The perfect image of God made into flesh, a servant to
creation, obedient to the cross; which not only represents death, but
poverty and humility as well. For Bonaventure, *kenosis* occurs within
the ideology of *imitatio Christi*. Which is a transforming work of the
cross, a freedom of choice that embraces the poverty and humility
of the self-emptying Christ in something more than a literal sense.
"Imitation by its very nature means expression,"[5] an inward and outward expression of the heart that is changed, transformed through
the work of the Spirit. This is a metamorphosis not dissimilar to that
experienced by Moses as he returned from being in the midst of the
presence of God Almighty. Or the imagery of Christ as he stood
upon the mount of transfiguration and before the eyes of the inner
circle became transfigured into an even more holy expression of the
Anointed One. Theoretically, self-emptying of the human heart is a
necessity in order for *imitatio Christi* to manifest wholly.

During a lecture at Washington Theological Union a profes-
sor, who happened to be a Franciscan, shared a narrative regarding
St. Francis. As the story goes, St. Francis had stopped at a monastery
that also served as a hospice for lepers to help prepare the campus
for an upcoming visit from a bishop. St. Francis made a point to
instruct one of the brothers to be sure to keep "those" people out
of sight during the bishop's visit. As he concluded his order to the
friar, St. Francis noticed one of "those" people out of the corner
of his eye; knowing that the man heard the conversation, Francis'
heart dropped. At that moment Francis called the leper to him and
asked the friar to prepare a feast. He then invited the leper to sit at
the table and dine with him. One of the instructions given to the
friar was to leave the table void of utensils. The leper and Francis
shared a meal together dipping bread into the same bowl of gravy

4. Evans, *Exploring Kenotic Christology*, 195–96.

5. Delio, *Simply Bonaventure*, 125.

together, one with hands covered with the sores of a dreadful disease, the other with a hand soon to exemplify the marks of Christ.

This story provides several lessons. One is very obvious; Francis initially acted out of his false self; that in reality is how most of humanity acts initially. However, once he recognized just what was at work he rectified the situation by allowing the Christ within to take control and the true self to emerge—a kenotic incarnate heart. The friar saw the Christ in Francis and perhaps even more importantly, in the leper.

The kenotic heart of humanity can be associated with what Cynthia Bourgeault refers to as the "divine indwelling."[6] The concept is that toward the center of one's soul, the center of one's being, there one finds the essence of the Creator. To clarify, Bourgeault quotes Thomas Merton:

> At the center of our being is a point of nothingness which is untouched by sin and illusion, a point of pure truth, a point or spark which belongs entirely to God, which is never at our disposal, from which God disposes of our lives, which is inaccessible to the fantasies of our own mind or the brutalities or our own will. This little point of nothingness and absolute poverty is the pure glory of God written in us, as our poverty, as our indigence, as our sonship. It is like a pure diamond blazing with the invisible light of heaven. It is in everybody, and if we could see it, we would see these billions of points of light coming together in the face and blaze of a sun that would make all darkness and cruelty of life vanish completely. I have no program for this seeing. It is only given. But the gate of heaven is everywhere.[7]

Nothingness and poverty are the genesis of knowledge both intellectual and intimate of the Creator. The One is "no thing" and though everything, exemplifies poverty, and is rich with love. The imagery of a diamond blazing has been well captured by Susan Muto in her work regarding St. Teresa of Avila's Interior Castle:

---

6. Bourgeault, *Centering Prayer*, 13.

7. Ibid., 13–14.

"The message Teresa communicates is both a seat of war, with moats surrounding it and foes trying to enter, and a sign of peace, with a diamond-like crystal of the soul in love with Christ at its center."[8] Each dwelling place, or mansion as they are commonly referred to, is veiled, and as the veils are removed by passage the metaphorical diamond or crystal of the one on the path is removed or honed as it matures, ultimately reaching unification with the One, or in St. Teresa's vernacular, his majesty. The central location of the heart for St. Teresa and Merton are essentially the same, not all will achieve maturation, but as Merton asserts, "heaven is everywhere." The issue is locating it. When the hungry stand at the corner or reside under a bridge, are they radically ignored or radically seen for who they are—human beings created in the image and likeness of God? The kenotic heart achieves what Merton describes as unattainable. At question is how?

Any attempt at humanity's identification of its own kenotic heart begins with its dependency upon the Creator and thus must depend on *kenosis* presubscribed. Kenotic Christology affirms that the first and in some ways most decisive phase of the self-emptying process is seen in incarnation through the second person of the Trinity, Christ.[9] In order for a kenotic process to occur God must change. The idea of a God who changes is difficult to embrace, but nonetheless biblical. One has to search no farther than the two creation narratives in Genesis 1–3 to discover two completely different depictions of the narrative. Perhaps a more rudimentary example comes from Exodus 32. The Lord is angry with his chosen and newly freed people because while he and Moses are up on the mountain preparing the Decalogue (Ten Commandments) the people are at the base of the mountain participating in disgusting acts and worshipping a golden calf. The Lord is so angry that he tells Moses that he is going to kill them all. Moses then enters into an exchange with God and reminds the Lord not only of the covenant with Abraham, but also of who he is—God. The conclusion of the discussion is v. 14: "And the Lord changed his mind about the disaster that he planned to

8. Muto, *Where Lovers Meet*, 25.

9. Evans, *Exploring Kenotic Christology*, 196.

bring on his people." The prime word in this translation is "changed." Other translations and revisions use words like *repented* (KJV) and *relented* (NIV, NKJV and others). The point is no matter what word or phrase is utilized the conversation Moses has with God delivers a change of action on God's behalf.

However, the Arian question remains: Is the Father greater than the Son? Augustine responds to this question with three illustrations in sermon 117. One concerning fire, one a mirror, and the other an image of a bush or shrub being born over water; Augustine's contention is that the Father and the Son are coequals and not coeternals, born of eternal begetters.[10] They are the same person, one being Christ, having two explicit natures—human and divine; however, Pierre Teilhard de Chardin would hold a third nature through the use of the term Greek *pleroma* denoting fulfillment or completion. The third nature is focused expressly upon the spirituality of Christ, which is cosmic.[11] In an essay "Christ in All Things," Chardin elaborates on the cosmic nature of Christ with the assertion, "We may say that he is and that he is still growing."[12] Some of today's Christian thinkers, such as Illia Delio, continue to bring forward ideologies conceived by great minds of the past such as Pierre Theihard de Chardin, who brilliantly gave birth to the ideals of cosmogenesis and christogenesis. Delio writes:

> By identifying cosmogenesis with christogenesis, Teilhard showed that the very being of the world is being personalized. New Being is on the horizon of already existing now; the Christ is present reality and yet before us, realized and unrealized, whole and incomplete. Resurrection is the necessary death awaiting us for new life to emerge in the cosmos. The old is necessary for the new; death is necessary for life.[13]

The emergent kenotic humanity is dependent upon the emergent kenotic cosmic Christ; both have to die to self to become compete.

10. Augustine, *Essential Sermons*, 200, 201.

11. Savary, *Teilhard de Chardin*, 205.

12. Ellsberg, *Pierre Teilhard de Chardin*, 88.

13. Delio, *Emergent Christ*, 90.

Christ accomplishes the task by first becoming flesh from the Word. Evans is correct in that the initial kenotic component for the Creator is to become flesh, where Evans fails is to ascribe to Christ the cosmic nature. It is precisely the cosmic nature that moves Christ into one of the more memorable metamorphical narratives of the New Testament—the transfiguration.

The transfiguration of Christ certainly conveys various exegetical variants for numerous exegetes, even the Synoptic and Apocryphal sources have difficulty agreeing upon the narrative and direction the story moves in. Some liken the experience to an unexplainable theophany similar to that of Moses and the bush that burned but was not consumed by the fire. Others posit an explanation of pre-crucifixion readiness with the certain three apostles—the inner circle—at the Lord's side ready to lead at the urging of the Father's voice. The passage poses problems for literalists, how does one contextually consider the transfiguration literally if the essence is cosmic? Perhaps one should anticipate resurrection upon witnessing Christ's being transfigured before one's eyes. If one accepts the *Acts of John* perhaps the entirety of the apostleship witnessed the event, otherwise only three were present. Nonetheless, one could contend it is the spiritual resurrection and the bodily resurrection rather than simply the resurrection of Christ being represented in the transfiguration.[14] Thus the transfiguration is an eschatological event supported further by Proclus of Constantinople: "Christ was transfigured to show us the future transfiguration of our nature and his second coming."[15] *Parousia* terminology not withstanding, the transfiguration cosmically emanates more than the aforementioned devices.

The countenance of Christ changed, meaning the being or image became other. Cosmically what changed? From creation to incarnation the change is seemingly obvious, but on the mountain in front of all present something else occurred. Arthur Ramsey offers this excerpt from an article published in 1931, by E. L. Mascall:

14. Andreopoulos, *Metamorphosis*, 19.

15. Cantalamessa, *Mystery of the Transfiguration*, 5.

> Just as, in the body of a living creature, there is no abrupt
> violation of the laws of physics, but rather those laws are
> absorbed as ingredients into the wider laws of physiol-
> ogy, so in Christ the perfect development from infancy
> to manhood does not destroy His humanity, but elicits
> its true function by rendering it the perfect organ of His
> divine self-expression to the Universe. The reality of this
> development is shewn by the Transfiguration. In the
> transfigured Christ the system of relations which forms
> His humanity no longer manifests it as subject to the
> normal laws of science, but shews it to be governed by
> new laws into which the old have been absorbed by a
> process of continuous modification.[16]

The motif of old and new again presents them within the context
of Mascall's transfiguration. Christ is becoming new in the cosmic sense through the physical image, but more importantly the
spiritual Christ has emerged as the One of creation who will soon
provide redemption through *kenosis*.

In Paul's Christ Hymn of Philippians 2:6–11, the text reads:

> Who, though he was in the form of God, did not regard
> equality with God as something to be exploited, but
> emptied himself, taking the form of a slave, being born
> in human likeness. And being found in human form, he
> humbled himself and became obedient to the point of
> death—even death on a cross. Therefore God also highly
> exalted him and gave him the name that is above every
> name, so that at the name of Jesus every knee should
> bend, in heaven and on earth and under the earth, and
> every tongue should confess that Jesus Christ is Lord, to
> the glory of God the Father. (NRSV)

Bruce N. Fisk put forth an article utilizing magnificent contrasts
between the writing of Paul in Philippians 6 with period Greco-
Roman fiction, at the conclusion of which Fisk writes, "Ironically,
the whirling machinations and interventions of the Roman gods
serve only to advertise their imperfections and moral weakness,
while the more restrained response of Paul's god signals only moral

16. Ramsey, *Glory of God*, 142–43.

perfection, unrestricted power, and universal sovereignty."[17] Moral perfection, unrestricted power, and universal sovereignty denote Chardin's *pleroma*, the completeness, fullness, and/or perfection of the true realized image of God in kenotic form. This is the image worshipped and adorned, the image imitated by Bonaventure, Francis, and Teresa. The image of the cosmogenesis, redemptive and exposed, the self-emptied, evolving glory metamorphized for humanity. Humanity must engage this Christ at a level beyond simple contrite theology and narrow-minded fundamentalism. In order for the kenotic heart of humanity to manifest herself through the wisdom of the transfigured kenotic cosmic Christ, the passion of a lover more deeply in love than that of a spouse must surface. Teresa of Avila relates this type of love accordingly:

> In the spiritual marriage, there is still much less remembrance of the body because this secret union takes place in the very interior center of the soul, which must be where God Himself is, and in my opinion there is no need of any door for Him to enter. I say there is no need of any door because everything that has been said up until now seems to take place by means of the senses and faculties, and this appearance of the humanity of the Lord must also. But that which comes to pass in the union of the spiritual marriage is very different. The Lord appears in this center of the soul, not in an imaginative vision but in an intellectual one, although more delicate than those mentioned, as He appeared to the apostles without entering through the door when He said to them *pax vobis*. What God communicates here to the soul in an instant is a secret so great and a favor so sublime—that I don't know what to compare it to. I can say only that the Lord wishes to reveal for that moment, in a more sublime manner than through any spiritual vision or taste, the glory of heaven. One can say no more—insofar as can be understood—than that the soul, I mean the spirit, He has wished to show His love for us by giving some persons understanding of the point to which this love reaches so that we might praise His grandeur. For He has desired

17. Evans, *Exploring Kenotic Christology*, 73.

to be so joined with the creature that, just as those who are married cannot be separated, He doesn't want to be separated from the soul (*IC*, 178:3).[18]

The "divine indwelling" place that Bourgeault spoke of and the "nothingness" that Merton ascribed to, are both present in Teresa's image of the spiritual marriage and exist in the love required for the kenotic human heart. How one achieves this love is a matter of both intellectual and intimate understanding which one might contend functions in relation to *pax vobis*—the peace of the house, or peace to you. The peace of the cosmic Christ is the central, calming, lasting hope of the kenotic heart. It is the eschatological presence surpassed by "no thing," lost only to the encumbered will, regained through the transfigured heart.

The mission of the cosmic Christ understood through the lenses of cosmogenesis and christogenesis creates a Christendom continually evolving, as Christ evolves, reaching a world with the love of a Creator for the created. More aptly stated, "Creator creates creation,"[19] initiating the universe from silence, to solace, to proclamation, to death, to life, to love—a kenotic love shared by both Creator and creation.

The world is full of injustices social, economic, political, religious, and cultural, to name a few. However, Christ is actively engaged in the world, seeking to provide light in the dark, strength to the weak, to turn the tables, even if metaphorically. Not necessarily by granting consolations, but rather by enlivening that "divine indwelling" place. In other words, the incarnate Christ living within creation, by relationship manifesting through an outpouring of love into communities—religious and secular—who do or do not ask for the love of God.

Today, the kenotic heart is alive in some cases. There are churches aspiring to feed the hungry and clothe the needy. Food pantries and clothes closets are becoming more abundant. Some settings are growing community gardens and feeding those who

18. Muto, *Where Lovers Meet*, 95, quoting from St. Teresa of Avila's *Interior Castle*.

19. Brueggemann, *Interpretation* 17.

otherwise would go without. These are meaningful and incarnational ways to serve the kingdom, but why should the work stop there? If the kingdom of God is the central focus point of what we do, and why, then would it not stand to reason that simply providing visceral materials is not enough? We should also be providing the eternal, even if that means welcoming all into our places of worship, or helping them discover a place that will spiritually feed and nurture them. The next chapter will focus on what moves and motivates our journeys. What brings us to a place of discovery, discovery that moves us away from exclusive language and into inclusive hearts and minds?

Reflection Questions

1. Describe what it means when the text says that Jesus emptied his heart. Have you ever thought of something other than surrendering your heart to God? Something more meaningful? More tangible? Describe what that might look and feel like.

2. How could having a kenotic heart help further the kingdom of God on earth? How would one maintain a kenotic heart?

Chapter 4

Understanding Desire

Whatever the expression, everyone is ultimately talking about the same thing—an unquenchable fire, a restlessness, a longing, a disquiet, a hunger, a loneliness, a gnawing nostalgia, a wildness that cannot be tamed, a congenital all-embracing ache that lies at the center of human experience and that is the ultimate force that drives everything else. This dis-ease is universal. Desire gives no exceptions. . . .
Spirituality is, ultimately, what we do with that desire.[1]

IN THIS CHAPTER WE will explore the fire that stirs within, the fire that moves and prompts us to act. No matter whether the action is selfish or selfless, there is something that causes us to act. Something rooted within our beings. In the previous chapters we have begun to discover that there is more to being a Christian than merely uttering a prayer asking for Jesus to come into one's life. We have also discovered that there is within us more than oneself at work. What we are beginning to discover is that both selves have motivational triggers. The more we know about those triggers and how to embrace or discard, the more Christ becomes incarnate within and without.

1. Rolheiser, *Holy Longing*, 4–5.

Consider the illustration regarding St. Francis in the previous chapter. Francis was initially concerned with the surface material ascetics of how the building and its occupants appeared in order that the bishop might be impressed with the work being done. He was reminded by the presence of the leper—who was the essence of the true work being done—that his initial thoughts were selfish rather than selfless, and quickly rectified the situation. The motivation for Francis was his "desire."

Desire is much more than a simple term utilized in conjunction with intimacy. Desire is with us from birth. Rolheiser describes desire this way:

> Spirituality is not something on the fringes, an option for those with a particular bent. No one of us has a choice. Everyone has to have a spirituality and everyone does have one, either a life-giving one or a destructive one. No one has the luxury of choosing here because all of us are precisely fired into life with a certain madness that comes from the gods and we have to do something with that. We do not wake up in this world calm and serene, having the luxury of choosing to act or not act. We wake up crying, on fire with desire, with madness. What we do with that madness is our spirituality.
>
> Hence, choosing certain spiritual activities like going to church, praying or meditating, reading spiritual books, or setting off on some explicit spiritual quest. It is far more basic than that. Long before we do anything explicitly religious at all, we have to do something about the fire that burns within us. What we do with that fire, how we channel it, is our spirituality. Thus, we all have a spirituality whether we want one or not, whether we are religious or not.[2]

Let's begin to unpack what has just been presented. Note how Rolheiser exclaims the idea that everyone has a spirituality and that that spirituality is born from desire. This is the highlight of the two paragraphs. How one engages desire determines the pathways of spirituality. For some the terminology is new and thus needs a

2. Ibid., 6–7.

bit more unpacking. Desire is motivational—it moves us to act or not to act in a given situation. For some, ethics and morals tend to be the causation of actions, and that may well be the intellectual extent without exposure to the realm of spiritual ideologies. Truthfully, desire is the original emotional constant that fuels the cognitive impulses moving toward an ethical or moral conclusion.

Desire is basic to all humanity—it burns like an unending fire that consumes our being. This desire invades our space, controlling our essence in such a fashion as to produce tragic devastation or unconditional love. Our response to desire is what moves us in one direction or another spiritually. Regardless of the direction, we never lose our spirituality. Our desire may well move us toward a Christian faith and we may well act upon that desire and become a devout Christian well aware of our inner self and the incarnate life. Our desire may lead us to a life away from Christianity and toward something more secular. We could become the next Jimi Hendrix, a guitar virtuoso, highly spiritual, fulfilling the fires of desire within. Both examples express spirituality. One lends itself toward the ideology of Christianity while the other is anything but Christian. Both speak to the desire that causes motivation to act within the lives of persons. It would be difficult to find fault with the Christian perspective, but how about the Hendrix example? Is it possible that one with the abilities to express oneself in the manner in which Jimi Hendrix did was not actually in tune (ha!) with the true self? Regardless of the answer one might have to those questions, the point is that both are examples of spirituality, one more destructive than the other. A third example would be the Christian who posits that he or she knows Jesus, but has no consideration for the incarnate living within and no desire to express the living Christ to the world. This case, as well, is destructive and occurs all too often within Christendom. The flames of desire are not squelched, but merely in the pilot light phase. Human nature is restless, always seeking to create life for itself. This is the effort of desire at work within humanity. What we do or do not do constitutes our spirituality, which will change as we traverse the intricacies of our journeys.

Desire Defined

For centuries humanity has struggled to define this massive term "desire" and all of its various functions related to human behavior. Plato said, "We are fired into life with a madness that comes from the gods and which would have us believe that we can have a great love, perpetuate our own seed, and contemplate the divine."[3] Plato certainly describes the concept in terms rarely considered normal by today's standards. One must consider the timeline involved— ca. 429–347 BCE—as well as the essence of Greek philosophy. Greek philosophy was interested in the study of humanity from an intellectual capacity—answering the most profound questions relating to existence especially: Why? Plato's teacher was Socrates, who was perhaps one of the greatest early thinkers known to humanity. A fair portion of the previous quote actually comes from Socrates' thought: "fire" and "madness" especially. Simply by noticing the dates of Plato's life one can discern that the mighty Greek philosopher was not speaking in terms of salvation, and actually not even in terms of the almighty God of creation, but rather of humanity's plight. Love was considered a Form of human reality, perhaps the highest Form, but not attainable without union. For Plato, "contemplation; its relation to love and mind or intellect (*nous*) and its source, the Absolute that Plato referred to as the One, the Good, and the Beautiful"[4] are benchmarks of critical thought. Exploring the dynamic further, "contemplation can be described as the way in which nous (mind or intellect), a divine exile in the world of appearances, opinions, and time, unites the two realms through its intuitive contact with the presence of the Absolute."[5] Considering the ideas related to desire for Plato and early Greek philosophy, while there may not be a direct correspondence to the risen Christ there are dynamics of human nature at work that directly correspond. The "fire" and "madness" certainly present a familiar tone of birth and stages of life. We enter this world in

3. Ibid., 3.

4. McGinn, *Foundations of Mysticism*, 24–25.

5. Ibid., 25–26.

a bit of a chaotic, if not maddening fashion. I recall the birth of my own two sons and the hours of intense labor, accompanied by the pressures of untold hours of waiting. It seemed that with every passing hour the phone rang more often and friends and relatives gathered like a small army preparing to leave for deployment. And then finally, the child is born! Immediately the desires/fires of his heart are clearly made known with loud cries, who knows what for really, just loud cries. And so his journey begins, much like Plato's cave, wandering toward the light and knowledge of the One with a heart to bring that knowledge to those who have yet to experience it. (A bit of poetic license is observed with the cave.)

Ignatius of Loyola (1491–1556), the founder of the Society of Jesus also known as the Jesuits, was once a fierce warrior and somewhat a debonair ladies' man. His life was filled with grandeur and lascivious activities until a gruesome battle injury landed Ignatius in a country castle being used as a hospice. There he was cared for by nuns and was given materials to read while he healed. Ignatius was an avid reader, particularly of romance works, but all that was available to him was religious materials—*The Life of Christ*, by Ludolph of Saxony, and de Voragine's work on the lives of the saints. As Ignatius became familiar with these materials an interesting thing was happening to the warrior. He was observing a conversion, a transformation within his own being. He noted that the books he once loved and held a high urging to read—romance book—only provided him with a fleeting sensation of pleasure whereas, these books relating to Christ and the saints truly touched his soul and provided meaning and purpose. All within the borders of these books gave of themselves to help others realize the majesty of God. This became real to Ignatius, so real that he spent the rest of his life creating a way of life devoted to God. He knew that the desires of the heart had two sides, one that worked for the good of God and one that suited the evil of humanity, so he developed a discipline of exercises to help those within his order to cope with daily life.[6] These exercises are available for all today, and his examen is utilized by religious and nonreligious alike to

6. Wright, *Essential Spirituality Handbook*, 160–61.

explore the events of the day and discover the weak and strong points, opportunities and those missed. For Ignatius, desire was a real driving force within humanity. One that not only had to be recognized, but also had to be dealt with—communicated with.

One thing to consider regarding the movement of the Spirit within one's life is that "each person's relationship with God is deeply personal, we are not always objective interpreters of our own experience. Since spirituality is essentially about growth and transformation, we should be in conversation with others in order to gain perspectives and to be guided in seeing where God is moving us forward into new life."[7] Wright is speaking of spiritual direction or what some refer to as life coaching, although spiritual direction fits the occasion more appropriately. As one begins to deal with discernment and face the fires of desire it is important to take on the heart of another brother or sister in Christ. Often our emotions play tricks on us and usually have the upper hand. When we seek guidance, by simply sharing our stories with someone, we place the chaos in the open and allow a neutral third party to listen to our hearts and provide not necessarily advice, but rather a clear picture of what we are going through.

Defining "desire" can be a perplexing task, for some it simply translates to the sexual aspects of life. While there is truth to that statement one must also consider the intimate narratives of one's relation with the Creator. That too is somewhat like that of a lover and the beloved—not in a sexual manner, but rather in an even more intimate, impassioned one. The following biblical examples will highlight several narratives relating to desire and one in particular that utilizes the language of love.

Biblical Examples

Certainly there are examples of desire that meet with completely secular viewpoints and compile a variety of carnal activities. While it may seem that actions such as these, which are driven by the inner

7. Ibid., 154.

being, are meant for those looking in from the outside of Christianity, the fact is, that is simply not true. The title or label one wears in no way precludes one from the carnal natures related to desire. A simple trek through the Bible should suffice. Consider the narrative of the Nazirite Samson. Born into a religious order so magnificent that the Bible names only three persons—Samson, Samuel, and John the Baptist—as members. Samson goes on to walk his own path rather than to follow the rather mundane rules of the order: drink no alcohol, touch nothing dead, and cut no hair. The young Nazirite breaks all those rules along with societal norms, as well. Eventually he finds himself in the clutches of Delilah, who finally convinces him to cut his hair. That seems to be the final straw and Samson is arrested, bound, and has his eyes removed. Perhaps the end of the story, with the Nazirite receiving his just rewards, but hold the phone, the band has one more tune to play. In an impassioned prayer to God for one more power-laden course of destruction aimed at the Philistines, Samson is granted supernatural strength and kills the lot of them by bringing down the pillars he is attached to and thus killing himself in the process. Within this narrative Samson, for most of his biblical life, fulfills the carnal desires of his heart rather than approaching the image of God in which he was created. He allowed the fires that burned within him to be satisfying, even for only the briefest of moments, rather than discovering the life-changing, life-giving, life-creating love of God to break free. Understandably, this is a look at incarnation through the lens of an Old Testament narrative, which may require a bit of creativity to fully embrace, so perhaps a New Testament example is in order.

In the Gospel of St. John there is a narrative concerning a Samaritan woman who meets Jesus at a well. The woman is there to gather water and Jesus is there because he is thirsty, or at least that's what the premise of the story would have one to think. Jesus asks the woman for some water and then goes on to offer her the water of life. She begins to question Jesus about this strange water of life and ultimately asks to receive it herself. Jesus tells her to go get her husband and the woman explains she has no husband. Jesus, being Jesus, knows that she has no husband but has had five and that the one she is currently with is not her husband. Well, she is living by some rather odd morals even in Samaria. The woman recognizes that Jesus is much more than a prophet, and is in fact the Messiah. She goes to her town and tells everyone she can. Some believe her on the spot and others come to the well to see Jesus for themselves. A great amount of conversions occurred that day. The woman, who spent a fair bit of her life chained to the desires of her heart, and perhaps those of others, had been set free to discover the life-giving desires of love found within a relationship with Christ. As that relationship had just begun even, she quickly became one who would spread the light of love to others by telling those in her community about the Messiah.

These two biblical examples provide a glimpse into the ever-present duality of desire. One final excursus should paint the picture quite clearly. The Apostle Peter, the one whom Jesus would build the church upon and the gates of hell itself would never prevail against, was within the inner circle of apostles. Peter, James, and John were the inner circle. Some contend that Mary Magdalene was also within that circle, but that's a story for another time. Peter was at every major event, even at the transfiguration. Peter was the most outspoken of the apostles, often firmly planting one foot in his mouth while swiftly lifting the other into position to join the first. Peter walked on the water. Peter asked to die as Jesus died, and he did. The oddity regarding Peter was that when Jesus was arrested and Peter was asked if he knew Jesus, Peter not only denied knowing Jesus three times, but also actually cursed the third time. Peter's desire to save his own skin played a vital role in what occurred at Peter's questioning. Ultimately, Peter and Jesus came together and Peter came with a contrite heart, one that had been to the inner darkness and found the carnal desire, took on and defeated it. Peter answered Jesus staunchly by stating that he did love him and that he would feed his people. The next fifty days would prove to be formative for the apostles, but especially for Peter. On the fiftieth day, the day of Pentecost, Peter opened his mouth once more. This time it was to proclaim Jesus as Messiah to all present as the flames of the Holy Spirit fell and some three thousand came to begin their journeys with Christ.

The final biblical example of desire that I would like to share is one that utilizes the language of love. This short book is rarely preached from, but does make its ways into the Revised Common Lectionary a grand total of seven times in a three-year cycle. The text is an impassioned one, rich with echoes of intimacy, this text is often left vacated as if God did not intend his people to read or teach from it. The Song of Songs, or sometimes referred to as the Song of Solomon, has been a source of much debate for centuries. Scholars throughout the years have considered the text in two basic fashions: (1) allegory, God's love for his chosen people; (2) God's love for the church and the believer. Strangely, this interpretation emerges from the mediaeval era, which most modern scholarship rarely turns to for solutions to exegetical solutions. The other form of interpretation most utilized is literal. So, perhaps we should break the text down a bit to gain a better understanding of what and why this beautiful book is not only one of Wisdom, but also one of desire.

As one approaches this text it is important to gather to set a framework. This is one of two Old Testament books that make no mention of God; the other is the book of Esther. An interesting detail, but not one that should raise a red flag, both belong in the canon. According to Renita J. Weems, "Song of Songs is the only biblical book in which a female voice predominates. More than fifty-six verses are ascribed to a female speaker (compared to the man's thirty-six), the experiences, thoughts, imagination, emotions, and words of this anonymous black-skinned woman are central to the book's unfolding."[8] As one continues to unveil the integral dynamics of the text, what is discovered is a lovely poem, or as some have contended, a series of poems. This is a love song written most likely by a woman of Israel to her lover and expresses her affections for her lover in the most intimate of details. It tells her story, and in some ways his, as they move from being together, to separation, and ultimately to rekindled union. Unmistakably, the poem is about a journey between two lovers in the midst of life

8. Weems, *Song of Songs*, 365.

during monarchial Israel. So how exactly does Wisdom or desire fit into this text?

From St. Thérèse of Lisieux:

> Do not believe I am swimming in consolations; oh, no, my consolation is to have none on earth. Without showing Himself, without making His voice heard, Jesus teaches me in secret; it is not by means of books, for I do not understand what I am reading. Sometimes a word comes to console me, such as this one in which I received in prayer (after having remained in silence and aridity): *"Here is the teacher whom I am giving you; he will teach you everything that you must do. I want to make you read in the book of life, wherein is contained the science of LOVE."* The science of love, ah, yes, this word resounds sweetly in the ear of my soul, and I desire only this science. *Having given all my riches for it,* I esteem it as *having given nothing* as did the bride in the sacred Canticles. I understand so well that it is only love that makes us acceptable to God, that this love is the only good I ambition. Jesus deigned to show me the road that leads to this Divine Furnace, and this road is the *surrender* of the little child who sleeps without fear in its Father's arms. "Whoever is a *little one*, let him come to me." So speaks the Holy Spirit through the mouth of Solomon.[9]

The language used by St. Thérèse is a similar form of poetic beauty as that of Song of Songs. She carefully beseeches her lamentations over consolations (which are the answers to whimsical prayers we tend to ask for ourselves, such as "Lord, give me . . .") moving toward a oneness through relationship with Christ. She cites the Canticle of Canticles, which is a nineteenth-century name for the Song of Songs, as a work that speaks to her soul. Many mystics—spiritual writers from the fourth century and forward—have cited the Song of Songs as a work that motivates the soul and stirs the heart. In St. Thérèse's case the poem moved her desire to a path toward the Divine Furnace and union with the One. Citing the faith of a child and the motivation of youth, St. Thérèse is sharing

9. Thérèse of Lisieux, *Story of a Soul,* 294.

her quest toward that which matters most—love. It is love that the Song of Songs speaks of—love for another that is the gift of life.

This love is also the Wisdom of the Creator that provides us with the ability to hold love in our hearts even when the one we so ardently care for is far from us until such time as we are together once again. Yes, the poem is literarily concerning two people in the era of the monarchy of ancient Israel, but there are deeper levels of meaning to the text, as with all biblical text. The Divine Furnace St. Thérèse mentioned relates to the very flames of desire that rule the heart and move the soul. Finding the place where desire meets the One can be a challenge, coming to a point when consolations are not sought for personal effect but rather looked upon as weakness, and is one of the larger and more difficult tasks of modern-day Christianity. Seeking something other than us is moving toward a kenotic, selfless heart as the lover in the poem did in relation to her lover.

Wisdom makes an entrance into the equation when once we have begun to embrace the concepts of *kenosis* and desire, and moved toward a more meaningful relationship with the One. Then we begin to assert new dynamics to our own spirituality's. Thus, beginning to become who we are—members of the family of God with roles to act upon. Our lives are truly our own, but are our own within the incarnate, meaning we live as the One who lives within, presenting the light of Christ everywhere we go. The responsibility is great and can seem overwhelming, and perhaps responsibility is a poor choice of words. Living out our kenotic lives as incarnate examples of the living Christ and presenting ourselves as the love of Christ to all we encounter should not be a responsibility, a challenge, a tasks, or a chore, it should be who we are. The next chapter will help us better realize how to act upon the ideals of desire as they relate to our spirituality in the world in which we live.

Reflection Questions

1. In the opening quote from Rolheiser he refers to desire as a dis-ease, how did that phraseology strike you? And now, after reading the chapter, do you agree or disagree?

2. Desire closely relates to one's spirituality; in fact, how we cope with desire frames our spirituality. Assuming this statement is accurate, describe at least one desire and relate it to your spirituality.

3. "We are fired into life with a madness that comes from the gods and which would have us believe that we can have a great love, perpetuate our own seed, and contemplate the divine." Discuss this quote from Plato. Does it conform to any Christian values?

4. "The science of love, ah, yes, this word resounds sweetly in the ear of my soul, and I desire only this science. I esteem it as did the bride in the sacred Canticles. I understand so well that it is only love that makes us acceptable to God, that this love is the only good I ambition. Jesus deigned to show me the road that leads to this Divine Furnace, and this road is the surrender of the little child who sleeps without fear in its Father's arms. 'Whoever is a little one, let him come to me'. So speaks the Holy Spirit through the mouth of Solomon." This quote is from St. Thérèse. Reflect upon the terminology used, especially the science of love, desire, the Divine Furnace, and the road the leads to the surrender of the little children.

Chapter 5

Acting upon Desire

Dear Jesus,
Help us to spread your fragrance everywhere we go.
Flood our souls with your spirit and life.
Penetrate and possess our whole being so utterly
that our lives may only be a radiance of yours.
Shine through us
and be so in us
that every soul we come in contact with
may feel your presence in our soul.
Let them look up and see no longer us
but only Jesus.
Stay with us
and then we shall begin to shine as you shine,
so to shine as to be light to others.
The light, o Jesus, will be all from you.
None of it will be ours.
It will be you shining on others through us.
Let us thus praise you in the way you love best
by shining on those around us . . . Amen.[1]

1. Job and Shawchuck, *Guide to Prayer*, 49, quoting Mother Teresa's adaptation of a poem by Cardinal John Henry Newman.

THE FIRST FOUR CHAPTERS of this work have been designed to take the reader on a journey of sorts, a journey into the realms of the spiritual. The first chapter introduced the ideal that there was much more to the essence of Christianity than a simple "sinner's prayer." We learned that our Lord wishes to be in a personal relationship with us, one that evolves over time. Discovery was also made in the essence of the phrase "let us create them in our own image and likeness." Along with the notion that being created formulates a role of dependency, but not one without love, we began to examine what constitutes our relationship—namely, desire. The flames that arise from birth that motivate and excite. These flames move us into our formation as spiritual beings and can either draw us toward God or move us in a direction away from God.

I recall an experience from the late 1990s. I was working with a ministry of the Original Free Will Baptist—Home Missions and Evangelism. My job was to set up the revival tent, which was a large carnival-style tent that could seat a few hundred people, in the small town of Calypso, North Carolina, for a week-long ecumenical revival. The tent was erected on a Saturday with the help of many in the community, including an eighty-something year-old man we'll call Buford. This man was there early, and for the entire week would arrive early to help me set up the sound system and other sundry items prior to the beginning of service. Mr. Buford was not able to lift anything heavy and not really able to do much other than drag a cable or move an empty trash can, but Mr. Buford was there with a happy heart and a sense of purpose nonetheless. I recall as the services would begin each night with some sort of music—typically, Southern Gospel or Bluegrass—Mr. Buford would make his way toward the front right of the tent and there he would very simply but happily move his head and pat his leg to the beat of the music. One night, very early in the week, as Mr. Buford was at the front engaged in his usual form of worship to the Lord, he collapsed to the ground. I immediately ran to him as did an off-duty paramedic in the audience who began to administer CPR. Rescue was called and a defibrillator was administered, all to no avail—it was Mr. Buford's time to return home.

The revival continued for the remainder of the week with many reflecting upon what they had witnessed.

Perhaps what could be said best is that Mr. Buford was living out the Christ incarnate. As he arrived each day to do what he could to help, knowing that physically it amounted to very little, Mr. Buford's light was a powerful gift not only to me, but also to those who witnessed his love for God and humanity. There was a special something about Mr. Buford that is not easy to describe, but if you were around him you felt it, that air of peace with the world and love for those within it. He loved with the expressions of his faith, which is a manifestation of the incarnate Christ.

Acting upon the desire that motivates our spirituality is what Augustine of Hippo was referring to in this infamous quote from *The Confessions*:

> "You are great, Lord and highly to be praised" (Ps. 47:2) "great is your power and your wisdom is immeasurable" (Ps. 146:5). Man, a little piece of your creation, desires to praise you, a human being "bearing his mortality with him" (2 Cor. 4:10), carrying with him the witness of his sin and the witness that you "resist the proud" (1 Pet. 5:5). Nevertheless, to praise you is the desire of man, a little piece of your creation. You stir man to take pleasure in praising you, because you have made us for yourself, and our heart is restless until it rests in you.[2]

This is the opening paragraph to his well-known work *The Confessions,* a book that St. Augustine wrote near the turn of the fifth century, designed to depict the struggles of life toward a movement of interior and exterior being while living in the midst of humanity's conflict with itself. The text is both prose and poem at the same time and causes tension among Christians and others due to its dramatic paradoxical style. For instance, the title itself—*Confessions* yields a dual meaning. One the one hand, it denotes Augustine's true feelings toward God as they have evolved over a lengthy period of time from his conversion to the point of authoring this work in his mid-forties. On the other hand, the work also

2. Augustine, *Confessions*, 1, I, 3.

exposes the many faults of the saint, not only those prior to conversion, but also those after. It is worth noting that Augustine cites
many biblical passages in his opening paragraph while attempting
to communicate his hypothesis. Perhaps one of the most interesting references comes from the most often Augustinian quote: "You
have made us for yourself, and our heart is restless until it rests
in you."[3] What makes this quote so interesting is that it originates
with one of the most mystic of philosophers—Plotinus. Plotinus
was born in Egypt around 205 CE, but spent a great deal of this
life in Rome. He became well known for his rapturous out of body
experiences and wrote extensively regarding union with the One.
His works are contained in six volumes entitled the *Enneads*. It
was within the confines of these works that Augustine developed
at least a portion of his formation. Bernard McGinn quotes this
passage from Plotinus:

> Anyone who has had this experience will know what I am
> talking about. He will know that the soul lives another
> life as it advances toward the One, reaches it and shares
> in it . . . it needs nothing more. On the contrary, it must
> renounce everything else and rest in it alone, become it
> alone, all earthiness gone, eager to be free, impatient of
> every fetter that binds below in order so to embrace the
> real object of its love with its entire being that no part of
> it does not touch the One (*Enneads* 6.9.9).[4]

The similarities to Augustine's famous line are unmistakable, but
note the most remarkable of the entire quote. The "experience" is
the union so often referred to within mystical writings and often
referred to within Plotinus' own works. Mystics would refer to it as
that time when one feels the spark of God, the very presence even
if but for a moment. It is likened to no other feeling, in fact, some
disassociate it from feelings altogether and equate it to the very
real tangible presence of our Lord. The pronouncement of the soul
living a separated life and needing to renounce all earthly matters
is very much what Thomas Merton speaks of in his ideology of the

3. Ibid., 3.
4. McGinn, *Essential Writings*, 45.

true and false selves. His contention is that within the human there exist two natures—one that seeks to live a life of selfish ambition and one that seeks to live a life of righteousness. Usually, and most often, the selfish nature wins that battle. In an earlier chapter the concept of living with a kenotic heart was explored. The concept of kenotic living brings one to a place where the earthly soul becomes one more in touch with the heavenly One. The heart, as Augustine so aptly designates, needs nothing more than to rest in the presence of God. Plotinus and Augustine concur on this major point, the heart and the soul combine—become one—sealed by the true self in order to permit the incarnate to be shared with humanity.

Living in this state—incarnational—is more than fulfilling. Operation Veggie Box (OVB) is a ministry that establishes community gardens throughout North Carolina. These gardens are maintained in an ecumenical fashion by local church bodies of various denominational backgrounds and harvest both in the fall and the spring of the year. The coordinator of OVB and his team have established a wonderful guidebook to ensure that each community has proper instructions related to how and when to plant. OBV also provides the seeds and plants at a very low cost to the communities. Each year thousands of people are fed through this wonderful project. In 2015, the group conducted their annual Operation Veggie Box weekend drive at First Christian Church located in Grifton, North Carolina. This was only one of the sites for 2015. At this site more than four hundred boxes of food were packed and handed out by several local churches who had spent most of the week preparing for the event on Saturday morning. The event brought people from various denominational backgrounds together for one purpose—to be the light of Christ to those who were hungry. For that one week of service, as well as the time spent working the gardens during the year, the incarnate Christ was present in each of the communities, being shared in a multitude of ways, regardless of race, religion (or not), socioeconomic status. "No thing" mattered, one only need be human.

So what drives desire to become something tangible, something manifest into the light of God? *Caritas*—charity; or *ordo caritatis*—

the order of charity. Charity most formatively translates to love. Biblically speaking as well as from a secular point of view, love has many faces. Bernard McGinn describes love, as described by Bernard of Clairvaux, as two essences: active and contemplative.[5] In a sermon on the Song of Songs Bernard of Clairvaux posited:

> But you, if you love the Lord your God with your whole heart, whole mind, whole strength (Mk 12:30), and leaping with ardent feeling beyond that love of love with which active love is satisfied and having received the Spirit in fullness, are wholly aflame with that divine love to which the former is a step, then God is indeed experienced although not as he truly is (a thing impossible for any creature), but rather in relation to your power to enjoy. Then you will experience as well your own true self, since you perceive that you possess nothing at all for which you love yourself, except insofar as you belong to God: you pour out upon him your whole power of loving. I repeat: you experience yourself as far as you are, when by that experience of love of yourself and of the feeling that you feel toward him, you discover that you are an altogether unworthy object even of your own love, except for the sake of him without whom you are nothing.[6]

Bernard of Clairvaux was a Cistercian abbot who lived 1090–1153 and wrote his most popular work between 1135 and 1153—eighty-six sermons on the Song of Songs. Perhaps one of the more fascinating facts concerning this wonderful mystical work is that the saint only made it to chapter 3 and verse 4 of the text. St. Bernard did not consider the text as most did exegetically, he gleaned the text in a more personally intimate level between Creator and creation. He saw the text as a means to a journey for the Christian, one which occurs in "places" and concludes with union. The three places are: (1) the garden—here the Bible presents the historical tenets of salvation; (2) the storerooms—which contain the virtues that enable humans to respond to God and restore their sinfulness to a right standing with the One; (3) the bedroom—this is where union with

5. Ibid., 525.
6. Ibid., 528.

the One occurs, there are many forms of union. For St. Bernard, in the Song of Songs the King represents Jesus, the Christ as the Incarnate Word, and the souls of humanity as the bride, the multitude of brides and yet at the same time the one bride, the reader being brought into the rooms created through the narrative as the journey toward union occurs.[7] The beauty of the journey is that the virtue of charity—love—blooms and the false self continues to surrender to the lover—God—everything to become the likeness and image of that which created him or her in order to share with glad intent the purposes for which the lover now desires.

In an oversimplification what drives desire is the shift from *our* desire to *God's* desire. Seems rather simple when we see it in black and white, and maybe seems as though we already believe that somehow we are on that particular path—if so, fantastic! Although I would imagine there is room for improvement in all of us. Human nature creates a paradox as Thomas Merton contended:

> There is a paradox that lies in the very heart of human existence. It must be apprehended before any lasting happiness is possible in the soul of a man [humanity]. The paradox is this: man's [humanity's] nature, by itself, can do little or nothing to settle his [/her] most important problems. If we follow nothing but our natures, our own philosophies, our own level of ethics, we will end up in hell.
>
> This would be a depressing thought, if it were not purely abstract. Because in the concrete order of things God gave man [humanity] a nature that was ordered to a supernatural life. He created man [humanity] with a soul that was made not to bring itself to perfection in its own order, but to be perfected by Him in an order infinitely beyond the reach of human powers. We were never destined to lead purely natural lives, and therefore we were never destined in God's plan for a purely natural beatitude. Our nature, which is a free gift of God, was given us to be perfected and enhanced by another free gift that is not due it.[8]

7. Ibid., 27.
8. Merton, *Seven Storey Mountain*, 185.

Admittedly there is a great deal to unpack within this generous quote. At first glance it would seem that the late Trappist monk was describing two separate things as he writes concerning the "paradox that lies in the very heart of human existence"; however, a closer peering into the reality of Merton reveals that he is actually speaking of the same thing. Our human nature and our soul exist as one and the same. The difficulty is our management. As St. Paul wrote to the Corinthians, he exclaimed, "So we do not lose heart. Even though our outer nature is wasting away, our inner nature is being renewed day by day" (2 Cor 4:16). Merton utilizes the language of perfection to describe the work of our Lord through our souls. The work being described is not of our own but of God, the Spirit working through us is the free gift mentioned at the end of Merton's quote.

Our lives are filled with traverses horizontal and vertical. Genesis reminds us, we are certainly not the perfection we some-times think we are; however, there is perfection at work within us. Merton is simply describing that work. At issue is our human nature and our ability or inability to release us to the divine. Neale Donald Walsch, author of the popular series *Conversations with God*, states the truth in this magnificent poem:

> Yearning for a new way will not produce it. Only ending the
> old way can do that.
> You cannot hold onto the old, all the while declaring that you
> want something new.
> The old will defy the new;
> The old will deny the new;
> The old will decry the new.
> There is only one way to bring in the new. You must make
> room for it.[9]

Our natures, our lives, our families, and our churches, are but a few places that Walsch is speaking to in this powerful concert of thought. We desire "fresh" in almost all the illustrations just mentioned. We want better work situations, we want better bank accounts, better

9. Walsch, *Conversations with God,* xiii.

looking homes, we want our families to be closer, to be happier, to be relational with God, we want our churches to grow both spiritually and numerically, to become meaningful to our communities, to worship and serve our Lord in more dynamic and meaningful ways, but in all these examples are we willing to dispense with the old and usher in the new? Are we willing to make room?

Richard Rohr describes the essence of human nature as something that we must die to, he equates the process to that of learning to love life by learning to die to it.[10] How one's human nature is lived out and who is in control of that nature is the key. What an awesome proclamation it would be to hear Christ say, "You are my brother and sister, and mother," but what would be even more impressive would be to hear the words "thank you." Turning over our human nature means giving everything to God—our hearts, our minds, our good parts, and our bad. It means leaving the judgmental mess at the door along with the self-pious indignation. It means every preconceived thought must be open to reconsideration. Ronald Rolheiser remarks: "God takes on flesh so that every home becomes a church, every child becomes the Christ-child, and all food and drink become a sacrament."[11] As our nature becomes more in tune with our Creator we become more and more the incarnate witnesses of our Lord to and for the world. The world becomes our field to minister in and harvest. We become the Christ that folks are seeking to see, feel, and know. It is our inner nature being renewed daily that provides the spirit of eternity—in spiritual and theological circles we call that an, "eschatological experiential being"—it provides us with the fuel for the journey of this life and the necessary nutrients for the life to come.

Over the years there have been countless examples of the incarnate Christ living through the lives of Christians. One need only consider the saints of the early Christian era and their selfless ways of life that led many to a martyr's death.

---

10. Rolheiser, *Holy Longing*, 82–107.

11. Ibid., 78.

Reflection Questions

1. There is a portion of Mother Teresa's prayer that reads: "that every soul we come in contact with may feel your presence in our soul. Let them look up and see no longer us but only Jesus." How would you describe the meaning of these statements?

2. In the Augustine quote we learned that the essence of the last line came from the Philosopher Plotinus. Describe how others have influenced your own spirituality; perhaps even others from another faith tradition.

3. The Song of Songs makes another appearance, this time with interpretation. What is your takeaway from the reading and interpretation?

4. Richard Rohr describes the essence of human nature as something that we must die to, he equates the process to that of learning to love life by learning to die to it. Describe how you understand this concept?

Chapter 6

Working within Communities

In the waters of baptism we are reminded that we are not born in a vacuum, nor do we journey entirely alone (although loneliness is often part of the burden). Being reborn, being made alive, involves being born into a community. So there are strings attached to this alternative. Far from being the spiritual journey of the solitary individual in search of God, it drags a people, a church, a nation, the human race, along with it.[1]

IN THIS STATEMENT, FORMER dean of Grace Cathedral, San Francisco, California, and Episcopal scholar Alan Jones nails the role of the Christian in the midst of the spiritual life. As one navigates the journey through nurturing one's individual relationship with the Christ, one must also consider the relationship with the communities—yes plural—that one engages. Certainly Jones has done an excellent job exposing some very obvious communities that one engages along the way, and they are well worth exploring along with perhaps one or two more.

Thus far we have focused primarily upon the individual as incarnate works in process toward the purposes of bringing forth

1. Jones, *Journey Into Christ*, 53.

the light of Christ into the world. While the intent of this work is primarily concerned with the individual, one cannot disregard the dynamics of community while exploring spirituality. Community is where the work takes place as well as where worship occurs, both exceedingly vital to the walk of a Christian.

Baptism into Community

We will begin with unpacking Jones's statement with a look at the first line. Here the scholar refers to the waters of baptism as they convey the essence of the Christian journey. Admittedly, this view may seem a bit skewed as it comes from an Episcopalian viewpoint, but nonetheless, there is only one baptism, be it as an infant or adult, one Trinitarian baptism. Consider theses few lines from the *Book of Common Prayer* that are part of the Baptismal Covenant:

Celebrant	Will you proclaim by word and example the Good News of God in Christ?
People	I will, with God's help.
Celebrant	Will you seek and serve Christ in all persons, loving your neighbor as yourself?
People	I will, with God's help.
Celebrant	Will you strive for justice and peace among all people, and respect the dignity of every human being?
People	I will, with God's help.

Prayers for the Candidates

The Celebrant then says to the congregation

Let us now pray for *these persons* who *are* to receive the Sacrament of new birth [and for those (this person) who *have* renewed *their* commitment to Christ.]

A Person appointed leads the following petitions

Leader	Deliver *them,* O Lord, from the way of sin and death.
People	Lord, hear our prayer.
Leader	Open *their hearts* to your grace and truth.
People	Lord, hear our prayer.
Leader	Fill *them* with your holy and life-giving Spirit.
People	Lord, hear our prayer.
Leader	Keep *them* in the faith and communion of your holy Church.
People	Lord, hear our prayer.
Leader	Teach *them* to love others in the power of the Spirit.
People	Lord, hear our prayer.
Leader	Send *them* into the world in witness to your love.
People	Lord, hear our prayer.
Leader	Bring *them* to the fullness of your peace and glory.
People	Lord, hear our prayer.

The Celebrant says

> Grant, O Lord, that all who are baptized into the death of Jesus Christ your Son may live in the power of his resurrection and look for him to come again in glory; who lives and reigns now and forever. *Amen.*[2]

Note the overall intent of the litanies—to love and serve. The first line posits the question, will you proclaim by word and example? The vow is not to simply proclaim the Good News of Christ, but also to live it as an example to all humanity—incarnate! The second stanza asks the candidate to vow to love all persons as yourself. Love, as we have mentioned previously, is the key to the Christian's path. Without it, we simply walk our own selfish way toward a dark and eternally lonely place missing the exceptional beauty of

---

2. *The Book of Common Prayer*, 304–6.

this world. The third vow extends the second by not excluding anyone and seeking to keep the peace through love.

The prayers offered over the candidates are just as vital, keep in mind that in an Episcopal setting usually the candidates are infants; although, there are times when adults are baptized as well. These prayers are intercessory and encourage the congregation to have a role in the formation of the candidates. Note the strong essence of love and life of faith given as a charge. Also, take note of the celebrant's prayer as it begins with the phrase, "O Lord, that all who are baptized into the death of Jesus Christ . . . " These are words of truth that have been used by many mystics throughout the years to symbolize the incarnate life of the Christian and the in-depth meaning of "taking up our cross." We walk the path with the crucified as lovers of the One who died on our behalf. Allow me to remind us of the words of St. Bonaventure from the preface:

> There transformed into Christ by your burning love for the Crucified, pierced by the nails of the fear of God, wounded by the spear of superabounding love, transfixed by the sword of intimate compassion, seek nothing, desire nothing, wish for no consolation, other than to be able to die with Christ on the cross. Then you may cry out, "With Christ, I am nailed to the cross. It is now no longer I that lives, but Christ lives in me."[3]

The language here moves us into a position of discomfort. For most of our Christian lives we have observed Jesus from the foot of the cross, and there is certainly validity in that practice; however, Bonaventure is positing a position of action, action caused by desire and moved by love. For the Christian who is living through baptism this becomes a natural evolution in time, provided the heart and mind are receiving nourishment. We will explore the ideologies associated with nourishment in the next chapter.

The second half of Jones's quote speaks to the unmistakable dynamic of community. Community is varied and wide within the Christian tradition, in fact, within the world. Community insofar as the "church" is concerned is made up of elements, including:

3. Delio, *Franciscan Prayer*, 115–16.

- Church
- Leadership
- Pastor
- Board
- Lay leaders
- Congregation
- Sect within the congregation
- ChristEasters (those who attend church only on Christmas and Easter)
- Outside
- Local neighborhood
- Local churches
- Local schools
- Local law enforcement
- Local firefighters
- Local stores
- Local non-churched
- Local homeless
- Local impoverished
- Local halfway homes
- Local troubled
- Larger community
- Larger city ministry
- Denominational outreach
- Volunteer services
- Youth outreach

Community is a never-ending component of the work of today's church. It can seem a bit overwhelming with all the "opportunities" listed above (and the list provided is short). For some, there may be items on the list that seem a bit bothersome for one reason or another; or perhaps maybe a job for someone else? Rolheiser states, "Jesus teaches us clearly that God calls us, not just as individuals, but as a community and that how we relate to each other is just as important religiously as how we relate to God. Or, more accurately, how we relate to each other is part of how we relate to God." Moving a bit further, Rolheiser goes on to cite 1 John 4:7:17: "He [Jesus] tells us that anyone who claims to love God who is invisible but refuses to deal with a visible neighbor is a liar, for one can only really love a God who is love if one is concretely involved with a real community (ultimately an ecclesial community) on earth."[4] The wording seems a bit harsh but the reality is that the life of a Christian, based on baptism, is to be one of love. Regardless of the formula used, provided it was Trinitarian—Father, Son, and Holy Spirit—the Christian is to live a life of love. So often we hear how inadequate we are, how we don't convey or conform to this teaching or that, or how we simply are sinners and without repentance we are doomed to a damning hell. This work does not intend for any of those reactions, but rather as Richard Rohr contends:

> Surely God does not exist so that we can think correctly about Him—or Her. Amazingly and wonderfully, like all good parents, God desires instead the flouring of what God created and what God loves—us ourselves. Ironically, we flourish more by learning from our mistakes and changing than by a straight course that teaches us nothing.[5]

Our communities can seem overwhelming, especially the ones we didn't know existed. The ones we feel convicted over are also challenging and can present hurdles to be leapt over causing angst; but if love is the center of who we all are then the work of our Lord can be accomplished. When Michael Curry was installed as the presiding bishop of the Episcopal Church USA in 2015, he made this statement in his address at the National Cathedral in Washington,

4. Rolheiser, *Holy Longing*, 68.

5. Rohr, *Naked Now*, 97.

DC: "If it's not love, it's not God." For those who know Bishop Curry you know that that phrase is one of his mantras. It certainly fits the topic of this chapter. We must learn to love, and our desire must be impassioned with love for God so much so that our desire becomes God's desire.

Biblical Steps

The Bible clearly establishes the role of the church by plainly depicting the role of those who become the church—people of the faith. In his well-known ecumenical text *Ecumenism Means You, Too*, Steven Harmon uses this text from Ephesians chapter 4:1–6 in *The Message* translation to open a chapter regarding "One Life with Each Other":

> In light of all this, here's what I want you to do. While I'm locked up here, a prisoner for the Master, I want you to get out there and walk—better yet, run!—on the road God called you to travel. I don't want any of you sitting around on your hands. I don't want anyone strolling off, down some path that goes nowhere. And mark that you do this with humility and discipline—not in fits and starts, but steadily, pouring yourselves out for each other in acts of love, alert at noticing differences and quick at mending fences.
>
> You were all called to travel on the same road and in the same direction, so stay together, both outwardly and inwardly. You have one Master, one faith, one baptism, one God and Father of all, who rules over all, works through all, and is present in all. Everything you are and think and do is permeated with Oneness.[6]

This rich text exclaims the essence of action motivated by desire. Note the compulsion to run rather than walk. If our hearts are so filled with the love of God and for humanity our intent to share should be natural. The writer of Ephesians concludes this text with an admonition for the Christian to remain unified. Unification

6. Harmon, *Ecumenism Means You Too*, 39.

seems simple when concerning the individual and Christ, but when it concerns a multitude of individuals with each other the challenge is great, sometimes unbearable. Dr. Harmon's book speaks in great detail to the nature of ecumenism, which means Christian churches working together despite differing doctrines for the causes and good of God's church. However, there are tidbits that effectively speak to unity within a local setting. Churches go through difficult period in attempts to remain unified. Some churches see numbers of persons leave over petty issues such as the color of carpet or the new hymnal. Others simply split over the same issues or larger ones such as whom to minister to: homeless, persons of a different race or ethnic background, or a whole host of discriminatory reasons. Harmon provides a bit of insight into unity or at least a means to put up with one another:

> Love in the biblical sense of the word makes putting up with each other possible because it is not a fleeting feeling that depends on whether we like the other or whether the other seems to love us. Love can be commanded in Scripture because love is an act of the will not merely an emotion. When Jesus commands us, "Love your enemies" (Matthew 5:44), he's not saying "have warm feelings of affection for your enemies," but rather "love your enemies in the same way I love the people who crucified me and for whose sins I have died." If that's true for our relations with our enemies and with those currently outside the church, how much more should it be true of our relations with all those who belong to the body of Christ.[7]

To realize the work of the kenotic church and fully embrace the concept as one put forth by Scripture, means to not only present the light of the world—Christ—to the world, but to do so without condition. Unity within the congregation is therefore a must. Every member must come to realize his or her role as the image and likeness of Christ to the world, beginning with the community of the church and then expanding the vision into the field—the mission filed that is the outer community.

7. Ibid., 45.

Our country was blessed by Pope Francis's visit in 2015. Millions of people traveled thousands of miles to simply get a glimpse of the holy man or to feel the essence of his presence; one family of five traveled 13,000 miles by automobile. What makes a visit by this man such a worldwide event? Why should people from all walks of life, all religious backgrounds, even nonreligious, stop and take notice; hang on the edge of their proverbial seats at the very words spoken, and watch intently at each action that Pope Francis makes along a parade route or as he walks past a group of people? One response is found within the pope's theme for this visit—family.

Family as considered from creation is a gift that knows all the dynamics of life. The joys, pains, cares, and emotions which represent all that is life, life that can be filled with the presence of the Creator even during the most difficult dynamics. Pope Francis exudes hope for all people by preaching and living a message of inclusion to all. He lives out his faith in such a manner that even those without faith don't feel the wrath of judgment, but rather a true essence of love for that which they are. His famous words "pray for me and if you are not a believer wish me well" demonstrate a real sense of passion for humanity. This passion is the light of Christ that all Christians should illumine in the world. Pope Francis teaches by the metaphorical Franciscan path—"Preach the gospel at all times, and when necessary use words." While a Jesuit by vocation, Pope Francis has chosen to express a true Franciscan spirituality to the world caring for the impoverished and the marginalized. It is precisely this spirituality that attracts so many people to his presence and makes the opportunity for evangelization available. All Christians would do well to take note.

Christianity is not about one denomination or one system of beliefs versus another. It's not about nor concerned with the primordial doctrines of humankind described to separate humanity based on supposed truths versus realities as prescribed by formidable groups of mostly well-meaning individuals attempting to contain the Creator in a well-fashioned box. Christianity is more concerned with the essence of God; that essence is love. I too have enjoyed the same experience as Pope Francis and have had young children as well as college students ask the same question and/or similar questions concerning not only where did God come from, but also, whom did God play with, why did God create everything, and the proverbial, who created God? While there can be no absolute response to any of these questions there can be one essence, and that essence can be none other that God is love. Why else would the One who needed nothing provide everything? God our Creator needs nothing. God never has, and yet God provides all things and does so because of one simple and profound attribute—love. While love can be a somewhat abstract term, one cannot deny the magnificence associated with the far-reaching bonds of love. God's love knows no limit and spares no quarter. For those in contradiction to God's path there is mercy and forgiveness, a means to right standing. For those who even fail to make amends there is no loss of this great love. Our tendency is to consider all that God gave up for humanity; however, perhaps we should consider that God really gave up nothing, but rather brought us into his world.

Imagine what it means to be invited into the presence of God. Not to say that God is somewhere other than here, but that God has chosen to invite us into his world, his place of existence. We have been created to dwell with God, to be in God's midst. So often we mistake the presence of God as our eternal reward rather than our earthly existence. God created so that we could be with each other in service and love not only to and for each other, but also to and for our Creator in his place—our world. Love knows no religion or person, love is simply love, it is the essence of God and what makes all creation work.

Pope Francis brought a message of hope for all humanity. A message that transcends even the doctrines of "religions" to radiate the true dogma of creation, which is to care for one another. Every community is dotted with the marginalized as well as the well-to-do; the healthy and the sick; the spiritual and the outcast. Thus what unites, or at the very least permeates, as a common thread is our humanity. We are all created from the same substance. We are all created from the same image as well. The love that is that image should be alive and moving through our communities as freely as the crime and poverty, and doing so without hesitation or fear. Doing so united on common ground with our sisters and brothers in heart, body, soul, and mind irrespective of the barriers established by humanity's institutional systems. Our communities need peace and love, period. Our communities need hope. It's time that the faith-based truly begin to work together to provide these beautiful gifts to all.

Reflection Questions

1. Recall your own baptism; what specifically resonates with you regarding your calling to a journey with God? Or what meaning does your baptism have on your continued journey with Christ?

2. In St. Bonaventure's quote he refers to Galatians 2:19–20. What do you consider it to mean to be crucified with Christ?

3. This chapter focused heavily on the concept of community. What images of community do you have? Have they changed? What would you do to improve the communities you engage?

4. Desire and love seem to be closely tied together. How would you describe the two and their relation toward one another?

Chapter 7

Maintenance

We are spouses when the faithful soul is united by the Holy Spirit to our Lord Jesus Christ. We are brothers, moreover, when we do the will of his Father who is in heaven; mothers when we carry him in our heart and body through love and a pure and sincere conscience; and give him birth through a holy activity, which must shine before others by example.[1]

THE FINAL PIECE OF this work revolves around the question of maintenance. How does one take care of the spiritual life? Is there really any reason to do anything at all? Is one spiritual discipline better than another? These are all fine questions and certainly there are more. The contents of this chapter will peer into a myriad of spiritual disciplines that help to maintain as well as evolve the spiritual relationship one embraces with God. Remember, water is necessary to grow a garden and therefore maintenance is required to nurture the spiritual journey.

---

1. Delio, *Franciscan Prayer*, 159.

Contemplation

The first, and arguably most vital, area to consider is contemplation. For years many have been taught that communicating with God is reserved for the high and mighty, and then for the clergy. Admittedly, the tongue is firmly planted within the cheek, however, there is a bit of truth to the previous statement. Self-centered pious individualism is alive and well in the twenty-first century. A colleague, a pastor of a medium-sized church in rural setting, shared a story about a family that visited his church one Sunday. He noticed the family, but was not able to greet them until after the service. They stayed for a bit to share their story with the pastor. Unfortunately, theirs was an all-too-familiar story. They were new to the community and had been searching for a church home. They had attended, or at least attempted to attend, several churches prior to finding my colleague's church. At every other church they had been made to feel unwelcomed. In fact, at the last church that they visited prior to my colleague's they were not even able to get out of the car before a man came up to the car and told them that they "were not welcome at this church." The family had decided to give it one more try, but if they were turned away or made to feel not welcome then they would discontinue their search for a church home. They told my colleague that "their prayers had been answered and they felt welcomed at his church." At issue was this family' national origin, they were and are Mexican. The churches that turned them away simply were exhibiting their own self-centered pious attitudes. They felt that welcoming such as these into their community was beneath who they thought they were/are in Christ. This is a classic example of how one's individual piety reflects upon the corporate piety of the church. In other words, how one relates to God—one's personal relationship—or lack thereof, directly affects the church—the body of believers—that one shares in a worshipping community of faith. Thus, that community, if similarly related to God, takes on the persona of each individual and lives out what light there is no matter how large, or in this case, how small it is.

In the above illustration the churches that turned away the family enjoy what can be referred to as a pious prayer life, but it is self-centered and biased. It focuses on the self and tends to exclude members from the family of God. It relates more to self and less to the community. The main ingredient missing is God. The joy of experiencing a relationship with God rather than something stiff and legalistic is never part of the equation, and thus, the community that is the church simply fails to live out its full purpose. Some churches spend thousands of dollars seeking the guidance of consultants of enlist the services of pastoral search committees once every three to five years in an effort to right the ship with expectations of righting the ship by a magic pill of sorts while the cure is, in many cases, in their very midst.

The church will always be the people! Whatever the church does or does not do within the spiritual journey soundly falls upon the spirituality of her people. The old saying "It begins with you" is more than appropriate in regard to the life of the church. The relationship each member has with God and the manner in which that relationship evolves directly affects the life and work of the church. The church certainly has her role to play within the spiritual development of her members, which is why seeking folks who recognize the journey as leaders and ministers is so important. Think of the church as an orchestra, each member plays a different instrument and just prior to performing everyone is tuning up at the same time—it's terrible! Nothing seems to belong together, there's no sense of timing or rhythm. Then the conductor steps up to the podium and strikes it three times with her or his wand, each member comes to attention and then the first right-hand sweep and the first row right begins to play, each in time and beautifully in tune. Then, the left hand waves and the first row left joins in, the timing is superb and the musicality is unmatched. And then, a larger sweeping wave of both hands as the entire orchestra joins in—pure heaven. This is how the church should be. Each member is different in his or her spiritual walks. Separately, we can sound simply awful, but together, under the tutelage of a God-gifted leader, we become something most delightful—the light to the world.

Removing the self-centered piety of the individual that ravages our churches with its poison can be a difficult challenge. However, it is certainly not an impossible one. This chapter began with the notion of maintenance, sometimes we have to build before we maintain. Discovering that prayer is more than something reserved for the high and mighty is simply a building block. Prayer is for all. When we pray we communicate with our Creator, we begin to enter into the presence of God in a real way. The trouble is that many times we don't view prayer quite in this fashion. We consider prayer to be a time when we ask God for this or that, a "Christmas list" of sorts and hope that we receive the things that we have asked for with little or no notion that while we were praying we were actually in the presence of God Almighty. So our prayer life is usually not all that it could be, or at best it's not what it should be. Contemplation will help us to better understand prayer. However, one must first understand contemplation.

Perhaps one of the most brilliant minds regarding the efforts of contemplation in the twentieth century was Thomas Merton; Merton wrote exhaustively on the topic. This is an excerpt from his book, which is a collection of essays, entitled *Contemplation in a World of Action*:

> The real point of the contemplative life has always been a deepening of faith and of the personal dimensions of liberty and apprehension to the point where our direct union with God is realized and "experienced." We awaken not only to the realization of the immensity and majesty of God "out there" as King and Ruler of the universe (which he is) but also to a more intimate and more wonderful perception of him as directly and personally present in our own being. Yet this is not a pantheistic merger or confusion of our being with his. On the contrary, there is a distinct conflict in the realization that though in some sense he is more truly ourselves than we are, yet we are not identical with him, and though he loves us better than we can love ourselves we are opposed to him, and in opposing him we oppose our own deepest selves. If we are involved only in our surface existence,

in externals, and the trivial concerns of our ego, we are untrue to him and to ourselves. To reach a true awareness of him as well as ourselves, we have to renounce our selfish and limited self and enter into a whole new kind of existence, discovering an inner center of motivation and love which makes us see ourselves and everything else in an entirely new light. Call it faith, call it (at a more advanced stage) contemplative illumination, call it the sense of God or even mystical union: all these are different aspects and levels of the same kind of realization: the awakening to a new awareness of ourselves in Christ, created in him, redeemed by him, to be transformed and glorified in and with him.[2]

Merton certainly offers much to explore concerning the topic of contemplation and it is important to carefully engage him from two points of view, one as a monastic cloistered monk and one from a secular lay parishioner.

First, as a cloistered monk concerned with matters of prayers as a way of life, contemplation is the way of life. Years of discernment are spent prior to taking final vows, which lead one into a lifetime of commitment to prayer and service to our Lord. Both men and women are able to enter into religious life and serve in either cloistered—meaning monasteries that do not permit monks or nuns to leave the grounds, but have roles that are rotated for one member to shop for groceries on a weekly basis—or in convents and houses. Those who are in religious orders and live in convents or houses usually are teachers, professors, or spiritual directors. These folks mingle with the outside world but still engage the contemplative life. They find a balance between the contemplative and the secular, whereas the cloistered have no need for such a balance, they simply live the contemplative. So what are the differences?

In the cloistered arena one is bound by vow, but really by love, to serve the Lord. In many cases this is much like a marriage. In fact, many nuns wear a wedding band to symbolize their marriage to Christ. This form of contemplation and awareness is mentioned by St. Francis:

2. Merton, *Contemplation in a World of Action*, 157–58.

> We are spouses when the faithful soul is united by the
> Holy Spirit to our Lord Jesus Christ. We are brothers,
> moreover, when we do the will of his Father who is in
> heaven; mothers when we carry him in our heart and
> body through love and a pure sincere conscience; and
> give him birth through a holy activity, which must shine
> before others by example.[3]

Note that St. Francis is not only confessing the witness of spiritual marriage but also the very real birth that flows from that marriage by the activities of those involved in such a deep and intimate relationship. He speaks of the unification between Creator and created and the emergence of the incarnated Christ through the works and deeds of the born again Christian who seeks the depths of the true self that Merton espouses, and finds that self by not only depriving the false ego driven self, but also by becoming the image and likeness of the crucified One who not only dwells within, but seeks to be born into our communities by our love.

Contemplation is a vital formational experience, not a tool, but an experience for the sojourner. As Merton mentions, contemplation is achieving realization of the presence of God within our inner beings—the true self as it relates to being created in the image and likeness of God. As one begins to discover this truth, the ego-centered false self begins to erode and die off piece by piece. Not that one altruistically becomes God, but rather, that one becomes the purpose for which one was created—to be one's part of the kingdom of God on earth and spread the light of the One that dwells within. To attain such a state of ecstasy or what others refer to as a measure of awareness, Merton asserts, "To reach a true awareness of him as well as ourselves, we have to renounce our selfish and limited self and enter into a whole new kind of existence, discovering an inner center of motivation and love which makes us see ourselves and everything else in an entirely new light."[4] Certainly one can correlate what Merton is describing with the concept of *kenosis*. In order to come to a point of selflessness,

---

3. Delio, *Franciscan Prayer*, 113.
4. Merton, *Contemplation*, 157.

to surrender one's ego-centered self to the true self that revolves around the interior presence of God one must, to the best of one's ability, empty oneself wholly to the crucified Lord. One may ponder how contemplation for the average lay person has any bearing on one's relationship with Christ and how that may impact his or her relationship with the community of the church and beyond.

Merton posited his ideology to both the cloistered and the layperson; although, it was with apprehension that Merton first described contemplative life for the layperson. Many of my contemporaries argued that laity simply did not have the capacity for contemplative life due to the influence of the secular world in which they dwelt. But Merton eventually saw things a different way and came to the conclusion that God did indeed dwell among all and that all were capable of contemplative life. A later scholar, Karl Rahner, once said, "The Christian of the future will be a mystic or will not exist at all."[5] The mystic, perhaps a venture for a future work, is certainly a contemplative. Merton and Rahner agreed that to love Christ is to contemplate Christ. A wonderful segue to understanding the gateway from desire, to love, to contemplation, to action.

Thomas Merton wrote about awareness and the necessity to become aware in order to discover our new fullness with Christ. Awareness is a timeless dynamic of spirituality. There are three classical forms of awareness:

- Ordinary Awareness—our minds as they typically think, with our sense of self closely united with that methodology of thought. Within this awareness the mind jumps from thought to thought, "monkey mind" as the Buddhists coined it.

- Spiritual Awareness—this awareness is likened to the tug one feels in a visceral sense, difficult to realize tangibly, perception is connected through an intuitive grasp of the whole and an innate sense of belonging.

- Divine Awareness—this is the point within the soul in which God dwells. There is in the soul a something in which God

---

5. Rahner, *Concern for the Church*, 149.

dwells, and there is in the soul a something in which the soul dwells in God.[6]

Awareness leads to inner awakening, which leads to deeper relations with the Creator. As one gains a handle upon each step of the awareness path the bridge to unity is being built. One journeys the path toward the incarnate and eventually finds the truth deep within the soul and relinquishes the heart, the restless heart, to our Lord and Savior Christ Jesus. The divine awareness is the rapturous realization that one has and is in the presence of God. As the journey continues, the inner path will lead to outward manifestations of that very incarnate being—Christ as light—to and for every opportunity that presents itself. Prayer is what ultimately leads one to the pathway of awareness.

Prayer is the overreaching path to communicating with our Creator. There are two basic or beginning forms of prayer: cataphatic and apophatic.

- Cataphatic—this form of prayer utilizes our faculties, engages reason, memory, imagination, feelings, and will. Here we can ascribe attributes to God in absolute language. God is within our understanding.

- Apophatic—bypasses the faculties: contemplative. Here God is never anything absolute, God is more than what one can describe. God is beyond our understanding.

Both forms remain necessary in the Christian's journey, how we understand, use, and embrace each is the issue at hand. It's not that one might move from one tradition to the other so easily. In fact, such a movement might prove to be rather difficult. Rather, some hybrid form of the two may seem to translate into a more balanced form of contemplative prayer for the layperson. Cataphatic prayer/theology tends to represent a more positive view of God in that one can ascribe attributes and sensibly attach tangibility to the Creator; whereas apophatic prayer/theology is the opposite—negative in that no such attachments are made, only a wider

6. Bourgeault, *Centering Prayer*, 7–14.

conception of who God is and ultimately not so much of who God is not. One should be able to posit the value of a hybrid form for laity as a means to drawing one into a better understanding of desire and more mature relationship through love with Christ. In some ways this hybrid form has been introduced without a specific name over the past twenty-five years or so, most especially in academic circles.

A movement of sorts to introduce monastic traditions into the general body of the church through course work in divinity schools and seminaries has produced the ability for the general laity to participate in retreats and small group studies that have brought the monastery into the home. These inroads have been paved by the orthodox settings and have more recently emerged in Protestant settings with a good measure of success. Certainly there have been some apprehensions, but as folks begin to discover the value of meeting God in different ways and truly feeling the presence of God through prayer and spiritual exercises the apprehension dissolves. Some of these exercises are:

- Journaling—daily journaling is a wonderful way to keep in touch with the movements of God in one's life. This can be accomplished on a computer—any electronic device—or written in a notebook. If one misses a day don't worry about it, just go on to the next day. Always remember that the journal is there, and when times of joy, turmoil, or discernment cross one's path, open the journal and attempt to find a place that speaks to the nature of the situation.

- Another form of journaling is known as a Cloud Journal. In this form of journaling one considers the shapes of the clouds during the day and night each day for a week and writes about the shapes and how God orchestrated those shapes. Write about what the shapes reminded one of, and how important or not that was during that day or week. Cloud journals speak to the Creator's touch daily.

- Daily Examen—this is an Ignatian experience and one will be offered in this chapter.

- Establishing a Rule or small set of Rules—St. Benedict has been considered to have been one of the first to establish a system of rules for an order. The task with this exercise is to consider a rule of life to follow. This rule should be a spiritual rule, one that is not easy and has meaning. The rule can be for a month, a week, or any set amount of time. Keep a journal while engaged with this discipline and refer to it often. After the allotted time has passed, consider a new rule or keep the same and move forward.

- Fasting—this is a biblical discipline, one that was shared by the Pharisees and the apostles. Consider what to fast from and begin. Remember that fasting should be a secret, so keep it to oneself. Attention to a journal during this time will prove to be fruitful.

- Divine Office—this is a prayer book, utilized by clergy in many settings but begun in the Catholic Church. There is a version in the Episcopal Church as well. Prayers are offered at differing hours of the day, for the early risers there is the invitatory at 3:00 a.m. and the day moves to morning prayers, noon, afternoon, evening, and night prayers. Special feasts days during the liturgical calendar are observed as well. These are wonderful tools for devoted prayer times.

- Silent Worship—this is a time of contemplation usually in a chapel type of setting in which one has the opportunity to worship quietly by various forms of prayer. One of the most popular forms is centering prayer. Centering prayer is a bit like Eastern meditation but with a Christian concept. One who is just starting out should begin with a 15–20 minute time period. During this time one should sit or stand in one place and focus silently—no music or any other sounds—on nothing. Having chosen a word or a phrase prior to beginning the prayer, each time one's minds begins to wonder to a thought one should speak the word, speak the word as often as it takes to bring one back to peace. The goal of this form of prayer is not to discover any brilliant revelation from God; in fact, God may not speak at all. The goal is to find peace within oneself. Peace is the presence of God. Do not be concerned with how many times one uses one's word during the prayer. Father Thomas Keating, who is responsible for helping to bring this form of prayer to the United States, was leading a workshop with some young nuns once and had described the practice and sent them on their first twenty-minute experience with God in this manner. After the experience was over one of the young nuns came up to Father Keating and said, "Oh, father Keating, I have failed miserably." "What happened my dear," Father Keating asked? "I had to use my word ten thousand times!" "Oh, my child, you did not fail, that's ten thousand times you came back to God."

- *Lectio Divina*—this is a wonderful form of prayer, which comes from the Benedictine tradition and can be observed in a monastic or scholastic method. A full description will follow in this chapter.

- Labyrinth—this is a wonderful way to pray in a contemplative format. This form of prayer can be done in a myriad of ways and no particular way is out of order. The general idea is to enter the labyrinth and move toward the center, releasing yourself—sins and all—to God. Once the center has been reached, then one spends time in the center simply adoring God. This can be done in a number of ways: raising one's hands, bowing in various fashions, kneeling, or simply standing at attention. The time spent in the center is completely up to the one walking the labyrinth. Once the center is left and the journey toward the entrance has begun, typically this is a time of drawing conclusions to that specific visit. For some God reveals plans for the future, for others God reveals a sense of purpose, or perhaps simply God's presence. For others nothing is revealed or felt, it's just a visit. The labyrinth is an opening to God and one's heart. What God chooses and one elects is the beauty of the experience. There is a formula where one may take a rock or several rocks that represent sin or some strife in one's life and as they walk toward the center the prayer is for relief, once the center is reached the stones are placed there as a symbol of God's grace and a knowing that God has the situation/s under control. The labyrinth is an amazing experience. Here in the midst of Johnston County, North Carolina, there are two wonderful outdoor labyrinths: one in Smithfield, NC, at St. Paul's Episcopal Church in downtown, the other is at Mill Creel Christian Church near the Bentonville battlefield in Four Oaks, NC.

- Solitude—Solitude is perhaps where we meet God the most. Those times when no one else is present; in the car, at home, at work, at church, on the lake, on the golf course and the list goes on and on. When one is alone, alone with the checkbook, alone with the computer, alone with the dishes, solitude is part of life and God is present.

When considering the disciplines of *Lectio Divina* or Daily Examen here are two outlines that may provide some benefit:

1. Scholastic Lectio Divina

   - *Lectio Divina*—Divine Reading

   - Reading—*lectio*: spiritual reading done slowly with precious care for the literal text in our hands or the uttered text in a group setting. Incense or other stimulants such as dim lights or very soft background music may also be used.

   - Mediation—*meditatio*: this is the process of chewing up the food we have just received through *lectio*. It nurtures our thinking side; we are seeking to hear what God is saying to us and to determine a way to respond.

   - Prayer—*oratio*: this is our opportunity to respond to God with our entire being. We pour our hearts out to him because he has just spoken directly to us.

   - Contemplation—*contemplatio*: this is the natural response to *oratio* where we internalize what we have just experienced and ponder what God has in store for us as we yield to his will for our lives.

2. 24 Hour Review/Examen—Ignatian

This may be done in the evening focusing on the day that just passed or in the morning relating to the previous day.

- As I look back at the day, what were the most significant events?

- In what ways was this day unique, different from others?

- How did I feel during the day? What were the emotional high points and/or low points? Why did I feel that way? Is God trying to tell me something through these feelings?

- How conscious was I of God's presence through the course of this day? When was I most conscious of God's presence? When was I least conscious of God's presence?

- Where did I experience joy today?

- Did I fail at anything today? At what? Is there something for me to learn from this failure?

- How do I need God to be with me over the next 24 hours? What events are on the horizon for which I need assurance of God's presence and strength?

3. Monastic or Sustained Lectio Divina

- This form of lectio is vastly different from the scholastic mentioned just above. Within a sustained form of lectio one practices using a portion of Scripture or spiritual reading over an extended period of time or perhaps even years. There are stages similar to scholastic lectio. And they are as follows:

- Listening to the literal voice of the text and studying with our logical minds,

- Meditation on the symbolic voice of the text with our intuitive senses (aesthetical).

- Heeding the moral voice of God with our personal senses of prayer and ascetical practices. The practitioner complies with the inner voice—through daily decisions and the discipline of discernment. Reception of the mystical voice with one's spiritual senses (this stage may never fully be realized).[7]

This form of *lectio* is usually reserved for monastics and others vowed to religious life; however, that does not mean that others—general laity—cannot be involved with this beautiful practice that not only creates a wonderful prayer life, but also enhances one's ability to exegete a passage of Scripture. One caution would be prior to jumping in with both feet either embark on a course that teaches this style of *lectio* or read a good text that presents the style in a study guide type of format. One such text is *Lectio Matters: Before the Burning Bush*, by Mary Margaret Funk.

Engaging any one of these spiritual practices will prove to be a beautiful aid to one's journey. Each one has the potential to draw one into a more meaningful relationship with Christ. A word of caution: while engaging in one is certainly a helpful practice in one's journey and maybe two would be even more helpful moving into high gear as it were, attempting to pursue three or more of these disciplines simultaneously is not recommended. Remember the journey is one of patience—a virtue—and should be treated as such.

The Fathers and Mothers of the desert, circa middle third to middle fifth centuries, these men and women sought deeper relationships with God than could be found in "church" settings within everyday congregational life, be it rural or urban. The answer, so they determined, was to set out to live independently among the caves of the desert. There these devoted folks could maintain ascetical virtues without the legalistic trappings often associated with the common church of the times. They welcomed visitor, typically once a year, as many practiced vows of silence to be broken only once a year. Their spiritual disciplines became banter for early tales and some folklore; however, as the "sayings" were discovered and translated, many scholars took them to heart, finding a good measure of spiritual and theological meaning within

7. Funk, *Lectio Matters*, 3.

their pages. Many of these fathers and mothers took on disciples, which ultimately became a foundational piece of early and current monasticism. When one considers not only patience, but also preparation to engage the presence of Almighty God, one can only admire Abba Arsenius. Abba Arsenius was born in Rome in or about 354 CE, was extremely well educated, and even rose to a senatorial rank. Once he decided to leave Rome for the desert he became a disciple of Abba John the Dwarf, a rather demonstrative charismatic soul. He later became a hermit and had three disciples of his own to mentor into the desert mystical way. Abba Arsenius was well known to practice the discipline of silence, but when he did speak—four sayings were captured and preserved—his words were powerful. However, one could argue that his actions were even more powerful than his words.

> It was said of Abba Arsenius that on Saturday evenings, preparing for the glory of the Sunday, he would turn his back on the sun and stretch out his hands in prayer toward the heavens, until once again the sun shone on his face. Then he would sit down.[8]

Obviously Abba Arsenius is demonstrating a great deal of patience, but not only patience, he is also declaring his love for God and the Sabbath. His heart is truly being worn on his sleeve! How wonderful is his expression of being? Abba Arsenius knows who he is in Christ and in creation. He considers the sun as it relates to the father and the larger story of creation in the new day—the virgin day for Merton—and waits with anticipation for fresh opportunity to worship. This is an example of monastic contemplation in one of its simplest and yet most profound expressions of intimate faith. The true self of Abba Arsenius moves from one God-given day into the next with nothing but adoration.

8. Chryssavgis, *In the Heart of the Desert*, 21.

Conclusion

Incarnational life is perhaps something that most have yet to be informed about—let alone consider. The introduction provided within the walls of this work express to the reader a foundation with which to build upon. By no means is this work an exhaustive composition on the subject of incarnational living. It is my hope that a flame has been lit or rekindled. There is much to be done in this vast expanse of fruitful harvest land. Every day more and more persons awaken the spirit within and begin the journey toward a truer self in Christ.

St. Matthew's gospel explains the very essence of what it means to be the light of Christ in the world:

> When the Son of Man comes in his glory, and all the angels with him, then he will sit on the throne of his glory. All the nations will be gathered before him, and he will separate people one from another as a shepherd separates the sheep from the goats, and he will put the sheep at his right hand and the goats at the left. Then the king will say to those at his right hand, "Come, you that are blessed by my Father, inherit the kingdom prepared for you from the foundation of the world; for I was hungry and you gave me food, I was thirsty and you gave me something to drink, I was a stranger and you welcomed me, I was naked and you gave me clothing, I was sick and you took care of me, I was in prison and you visited me." Then the righteous will answer him, "Lord, when was it that we saw you hungry and gave you food, or thirsty and gave you something to drink? And when was it that we saw you a stranger and welcomed you, or naked and gave you clothing? And when was it that we saw you sick or in prison and visited you?" And the king will answer them, "Truly I tell you, just as you did it to one of the least of these who are members of my family, you did it to me." Then he will say to those at his left hand, "You that are accursed, depart from me into the eternal fire prepared for the devil and his angels; for I was hungry and you gave me no food, I was thirsty and you gave me nothing to drink, I was a stranger and you did not welcome

me, naked and you did not give me clothing, sick and in prison and you did not visit me." Then they also will answer, "Lord, when was it that we saw you hungry or thirsty or a stranger or naked or sick or in prison, and did not take care of you?" Then he will answer them, "Truly I tell you, just as you did not do it to one of the least of these, you did not do it to me." And these will go away into eternal punishment, but the righteous into eternal life. (Matt 25:31–46)

These words were spoken not to the unfaithful, but to the faithful in Christ. It is and will always be the purpose of the faithful in Christ to cloth the naked, feed the hungry, take care of the sick, and be the light of Christ to all.

The reason for this book is to help nurture and offer a means of preparation toward a more fruitful expression of one's relationship with God. By discovering that there exists much more than a simple prayer of salvation in the journey of faith, one begins to realize that the cross, which we are asked to bear by Jesus daily, has personal implications. Those implications reach deeply into the human soul, which is truly not our own, but God's. The essence of this work has been to help discover the meaning of the true and false self and just how desire plays a major role in which self ultimately controls one's being. Once one recognizes this paradoxical lifelong situation, one has the ability to function in the capacity of *imitatio Christi*—image of Christ—that one has been created toward. Our communities are in dire need of experiencing the Christ of our hearts, the one that dwells within our souls and unleashes the true self of our being. It is our purpose to make that happen regardless of race, religion, socioeconomic status, gender, or sexual orientation. People are God's creation, all people, and as followers of God, carriers of the incarnate Christ, we are to love as God does—with our whole heart and without condition. That is kenotic expression at its ultimate fruition. Reaching back to the desert fathers and mothers:

Abba Nistheros the Great asked Abba Anthony, What good work should I be doing? He said to him: "Are not all actions equal? Scripture says that Abraham was hospitable, and God was with him. David was humble, and God was with him. Elias loved interior peace, and God was with him. So, do whatever you see that your soul desires according to God, and guard your heart."[9]

Reflection Questions

1. The opening statement from St. Francis contends that the spiritual life is a symbolic marriage with God, and many other mystics and spiritual folks across the years have utilized this type of language to describe the spiritual life. How does this language sit with you?

2. What does the term *contemplation* mean to you?

3. Express how one's spiritual life affects the spiritual life of the church.

4. Are there boundaries to the reach of the love of Christ? Regardless of the response, explain. As an individual, does one have these same boundaries? Explain.

9. Ibid., 13.

Bibliography

Andreopoulos, Andreas. *Metamorphosis: The Transfiguration in Byzantine Iconography*. Crestwood: St. Vladimir's Seminary Press, 2005.

Augustine. *Confessions*. Translated by Henry Chadwick. New York: Oxford University Press, 2008.

————. *Essential Sermons*. The Works of Saint Augustine: A Translation for the 21st Century 3. Edited by Boniface Ramsey. Translated by Edmund Hill. Hyde Park: New City, 2007.

Bourgeault, Cynthia. *Centering Prayer and Inner Awakening*. Cambridge: Cowley, 2004.

Brueggemann, Walter. *Genesis*. Interpretation: A Bible Commentary for Teaching and Preaching. Louisville: Westminster John Knox, 2010.

Cantalamessa, Raniero. *The Mystery of the Transfiguration*. Translated by Marsha Daigle-Willamson. Cincinnati: St. Anthony Messenger, 2008.

Chryssavgis, John. *In the Heart of the Desert: The Spirituality of the Desert Fathers and Mothers*. Rev. ed. Bloomington: World Wisdom, 2008.

Delio, Ilia. *Clare of Assisi: A Heart Full of Love*. Cincinnati: St. Anthony Messenger Press, 2007.

————. *The Emergent Christ: Exploring the Meaning of Catholic on an Evolutionary Universe*. Maryknoll: Orbis, 2011.

————. *Franciscan Prayer*. Cincinnati: St. Anthony Messenger Press, 2004.

————. *Simply Bonaventure: An Introduction to His Life, Thought, and Writings*. Hyde Park: New City, 2001.

Ellsberg, Robert, ed. *Pierre Teilhard de Chardin: Writings*. Modern Spiritual Masters. Maryknoll: Orbis, 1999.

Evans, C. Stephen, ed. *Exploring Kenotic Christology: The Self-Emptying of God*. Vancouver: Regent College Press, 2006.

Foley, Marc, ed. *The Ascent to Joy: John of the Cross, Selected Spiritual Writings*. Hyde Park: New City, 2002.

Funk, Mary Margaret. *Lectio Matters: Before the Burning Bush; Through the Revelatory Texts of Scripture, Nature and Experience.* New York: Continuum, 2010.

Harmon, Steven R. *Ecumenism Means You, Too.* Eugene, OR: Cascade, 2010.

Job, Rueben P., and Norman Shawchuck. *A Guide to Prayer for All God's People.* Nashville: Upper Room, 1990.

Jones, Alan. *Journey Into Christ.* New York: Seabury, 1977.

Lincoln, Andrew T. *The New Interpreter's Bible: A Commentary in Twelve Volumes.* Vol. 11. Nashville: Abingdon, 2000.

Lull, Ramón. *The Book of the Lover and the Beloved.* Translated by Allison Peers. Edited by Kenneth Leech. New York: Paulist, 1978.

McGinn, Bernard, ed. *The Essential Writings of Christian Mysticism.* New York: Modern Library, 2006.

———. *The Foundations of Mysticism: Origins to the Fifth Century.* New York: Crossroad, 1991.

Merton, Thomas. *Conjectures of a Guilty Bystander.* New York: Image, 2014.

———. *Contemplation in a World of Action.* Notre Dame: University of Notre Dame Press, 1998.

———. *The Seven Storey Mountain: An Autobiography of Faith.* New York: Harvest, 1976.

Muto, Susan. *Where Lovers Meet: Inside the Interior Castle.* Washington, DC: ICS, 2008.

Rahner, Karl. *Concern for the Church.* Theological Investigations 20. New York: Crossroad, 1981.

Ramsey, Arthur Michael. *The Glory of God and the Transfiguration of Christ.* Eugene, OR: Wipf & Stock, 2009.

Rohr, Richard. *The Naked Now: Learning to See as the Mystics See.* New York: Crossroad, 2009.

Rolheiser, Roland. *The Holy Longing: The Search for a Christian Spirituality.* New York: Doubleday, 1999.

Savary, Louis M. *Teilhard de Chardin: The Divine Milieu Explained; A Spirituality for the 21st Century.* Mahwah, NJ: Paulist, 2007.

Teresa of Avila. *The Interior Castle.* Vol. 2. Translated by Kieran Kavanaugh. The Collected Works of St. Teresa of Avila. Washington, DC: ICS, 1980.

Thérèse of Lisieux. *Story of a Soul.* Translated by John Clarke. Prepared by Mark Foley. Study ed. Washington, DC: ICS, 2005.

Walsch, Neale Donald. *Conversations with God: An Uncommon Dialogue.* Book 1. New York: Putman, 1995.

Weems, Renita J. *Song of Songs.* In *The New Interpreter's Bible*, vol. 5, edited by Raymond C. Van Leeuwen. Nashville: Abingdon, 1997.

Wright, Wendy M. *The Essential Spirituality Handbook.* Liguori, MO: Liguori, 2009.

www.ingramcontent.com/pod-product-compliance
Lightning Source LLC
Chambersburg PA
CBHW060422090426
42734CB00011B/2406